The Storyteller

Claire Gilman and Margaret Sundell (eds.)
Independent Curators International

jrp|ringier

Table of Contents

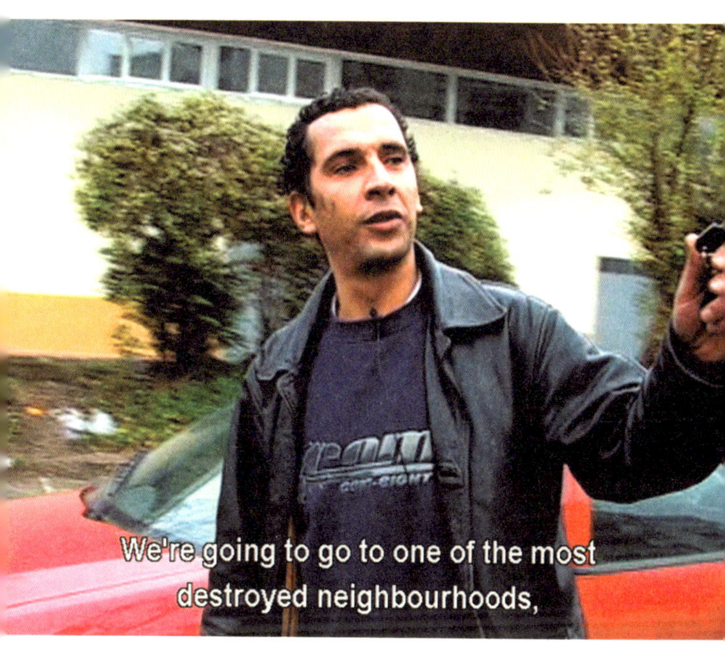

We're going to go to one of the most
destroyed neighbourhoods,

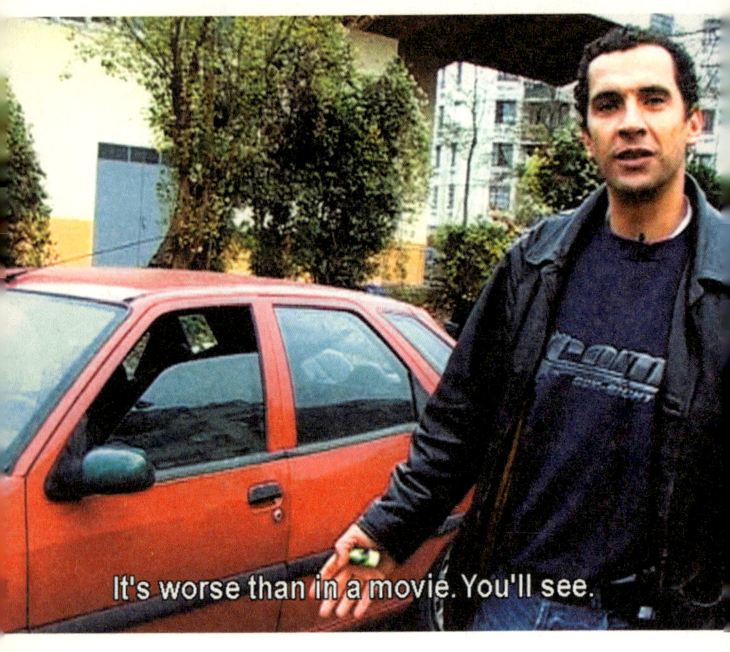

← ↑ EMANUEL LICHA, *War Tourist in the Suburbs of Paris*, 2004–2008 (video stills)

MISSING BOOKS, *Un Oscuro Día de Justicia (A Dark Day of Justice)*, 2005 (installation view, Scheltema Complex, Leiden, The Netherlands) → → → → →

The Storyteller
Claire Gilman and Margaret Sundell

[The Story] does not aim to convey the pure essence of the thing, like information or a report. It sinks the thing into the life of the storyteller, in order to bring it out of him again. The traces of the storyteller cling to the story the way the handprints of the potter cling to the clay vessel.
—Walter Benjamin, "The Storyteller," 1936[1]

Shifts within the aesthetic realm can never be fully explained by events in the world. Still, it is hard not to connect the documentary impulse that marks much recent artistic production—what is often referred to as art's "documentary turn"—to the pressures exerted by the rapid, often violent transformations of the last few decades, from the post-Soviet reconstruction of Eastern Europe to the outbreak of war in Iraq. Faced with a reality fraught with global conflict, artists are increasingly seeking to respond to and come to terms with the world around them. *The Storyteller* isolates an overlooked yet vital strand within this broader tendency: the use of the story form as a means of comprehending and conveying recent social and political events.

In this effort, *The Storyteller's* artists build on an earlier aesthetic shift often referred to as postmodernism, which challenged the basic principles (as articulated by critic Clement Greenberg) of modernist art, notably its ban on narrative and representational content and insistence on art's autonomy from everyday life. Modernism's reductive and empiricist orientation—its drive to attain underlying essences and to ground those ideals in the certainty of material fact—was equally an object of critique. However, unlike their postmodern predecessors such as Cindy Sherman or Richard Prince, who turned to artifice and disguise as a way of challenging the existence of singular, irrevocable truths and asserting the constructed nature of the self, the artists featured here are not content to explore the ideological implications of modernism's quest for absolutes. Their work strives less to dismantle the category of objective truth or to abandon fact for fabulation than to establish an authentic connection to reality that acknowledges the inevitably subjective nature of this relationship.

As T.J. Demos suggests in his essay "Storytelling in/as Contemporary Art," given the story form's association with fiction and childhood fantasy, an affiliation with documentary practice might initially seem counterintuitive. But the artists in question are deeply engaged with the realities of their historical contexts. Indeed, all the works in the exhibition revolve around real-life situations. In each case, however, these events are re-imagined and thereby re-experienced through the artist's personal encounter or the character's narration. The exhibition features artists from all over the world, working in a variety of media. In some cases, the artist's "story" takes the form of an invented drama based on real events; in others, an appeal to universalizing literary genres such as the fairytale or the quest; in still others, a dialogue or communicative exchange between active participants in a contemporary political situation. But in all instances, the artists adopt the story's use of commonly shared tropes to unite individual circumstances with communal histories. The truth that storytelling conveys is not that of facts—although specific places and events necessarily emerge in the telling—but of experience with all the contingency, uncertainty, and partiality that this term implies.

If storytelling permits a different kind of truth, it also necessitates a particular worldview, one in which action is tempered by reflection. Indeed, by its very nature, storytelling implies that things are never resolved once and for all. Instead, events are taken up, digested, and reformulated through the listener's interpretive process and through each subsequent retelling. Storytelling is in this way a fundamentally egalitarian form.[2] One might even go so far as to say that storytelling is a form for our times. Or at least it would seem to be ever more urgently needed in today's increasingly global but still fragmented world. What must be reclaimed is that fundamental attribute of storytelling—the exchange of experiences—which Walter Benjamin saw as disappearing from the horizon over a half century ago. Writing in 1936, Benjamin lamented, "the art of storytelling is coming to an end."[3] In projecting its demise, he specifically saw storytelling as being superseded by then new forms of journalism and mass media, such as newsreels and photojournalism, that, in lieu of epic truths and shared wisdom, emphasized verifiable and immediately graspable facts. In their marriage of story and document, the works in this exhibition aim to move beyond precisely this dichotomy.

French philosopher Paul Ricoeur observed that stories are essentially tri-partite in nature. There is the experience stories recount, the form in which it is delivered, and the refiguring of this

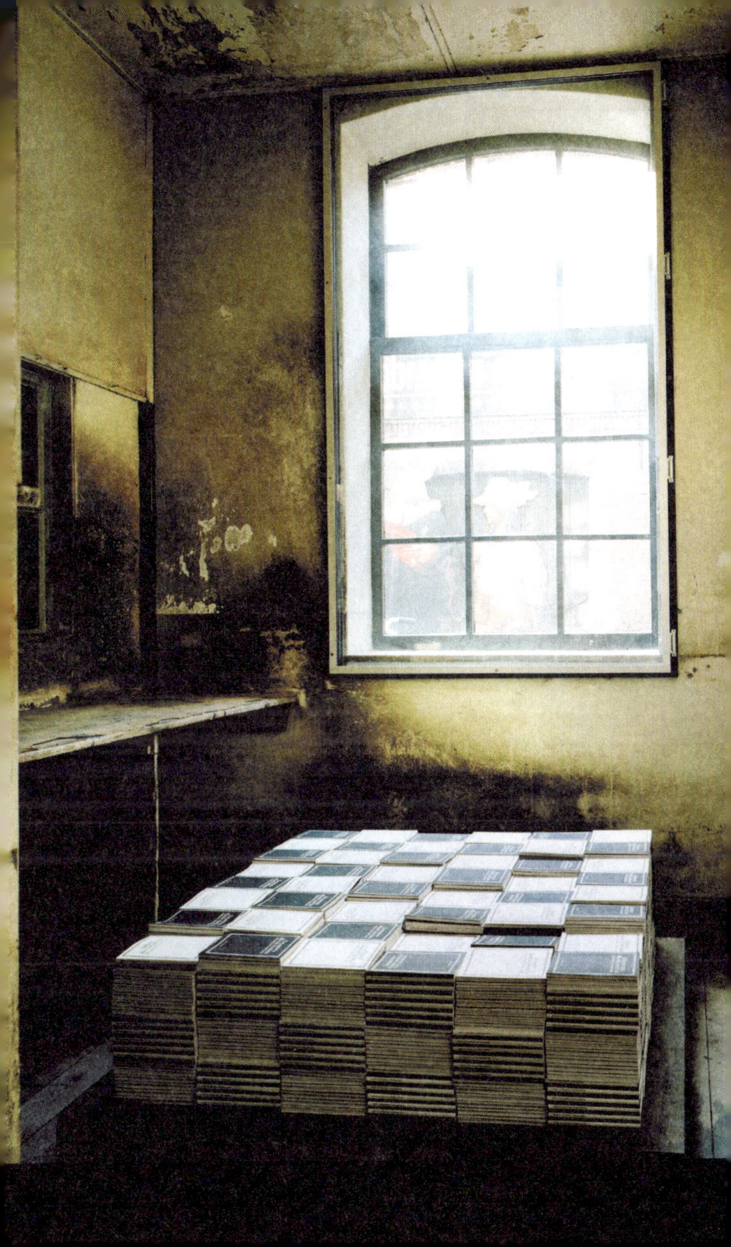

narrative by the receiver—in whose hands, naturally, the process resumes.[4] While every story inevitably contains elements of all three modes, in what follows we have divided the artists in the exhibition according to the above-mentioned categories: experience, form, and reception. We hope in this way to focus attention both on the particular concerns of the work at hand and, more broadly, on the way in which stories move—from event to experience; from experience to narrative; from one person to another.

The Truth of Experience

"The storyteller," Benjamin wrote, "takes what he tells from experience [...] And he in turn makes it the experience of those who are listening to his tale."[5] For many of the artists in this exhibition, this capacity of storytelling is specifically linked to an experience of place as the ground of a past event that continues to shape the present. The site remains charged with the energy of its past, which the story serves to re-activate. What results is not simply the recovery of the memory associated with the site, but an interweaving of its present and past through the story's connective tissue. Exemplary in this regard is Emanuel Licha's *War Tourist in the*

Suburbs of Paris, one in a series of videos of sites of war or disaster that Licha surveys with a local guide—as tourists do when visiting exotic landmarks or ancient ruins. But here, the Canadian artist (who divides his time between Montreal and Paris) travels no further than his own backyard: the outskirts of the French capital in the aftermath of the 2005 riots. The guide points out his former home (a building destroyed in the riots) and the mosque that was teargassed by the police. He takes Licha to see abandoned buildings covered with graffiti and the neighborhood soccer field where he played as a boy that the government paved over to serve as a parking lot. Along the way he suggests that the violence that erupted here was less retribution for the deaths of two local teens at the hands of the police than an expression of the pent-up economic and racial frustrations of the neighborhood's mostly poor, black Muslim inhabitants; his official "tour" transforms into a heartfelt story, an impassioned account of lived experience.

The story's ability to access a past embodied in a particular site similarly occupies *In the Last 20 Minutes* by the Missing Books collective (Maxine Kopsa, Germaine Kruip, and Maria Barnas). Filmed on location in Buenos Aires, the

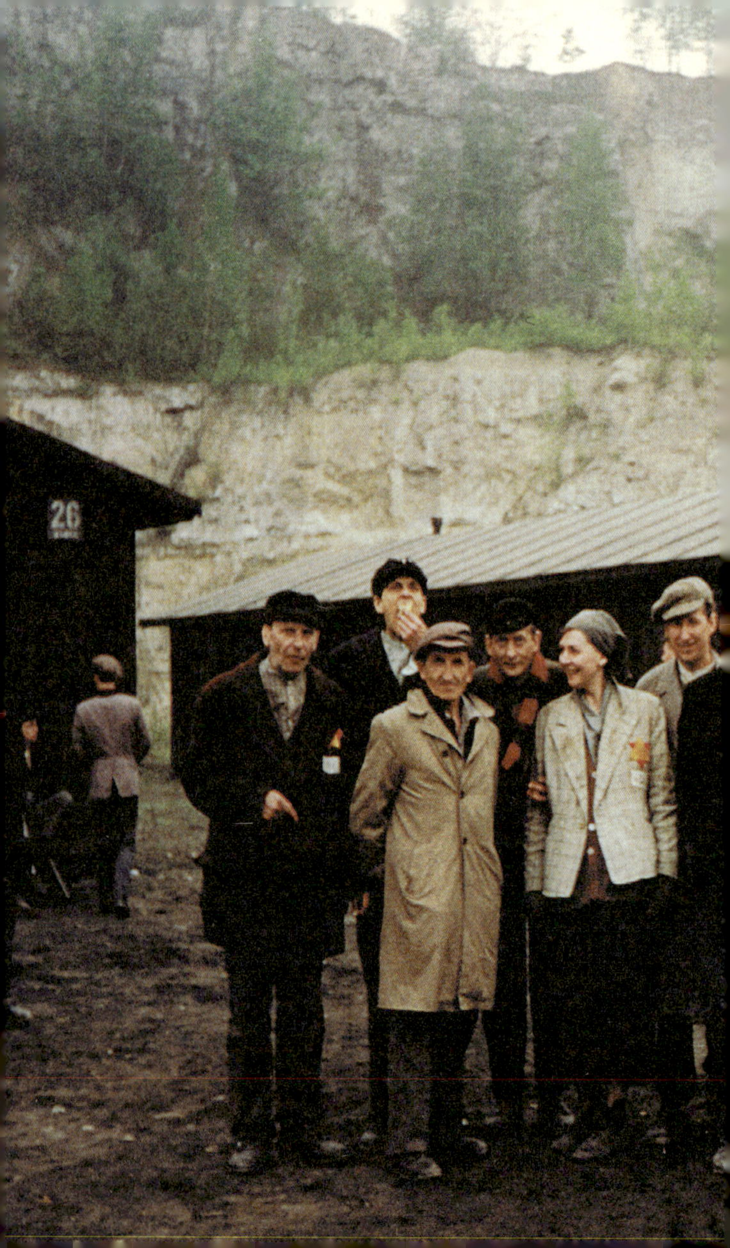

26

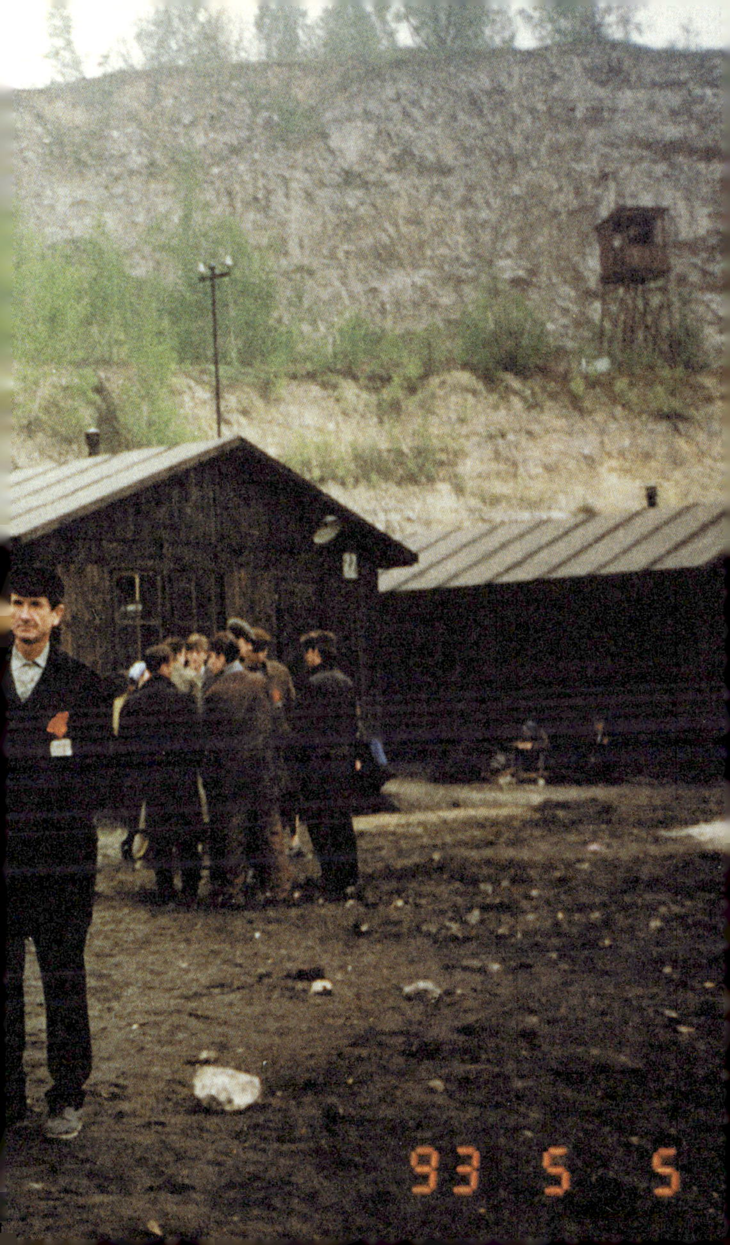
93 5 5

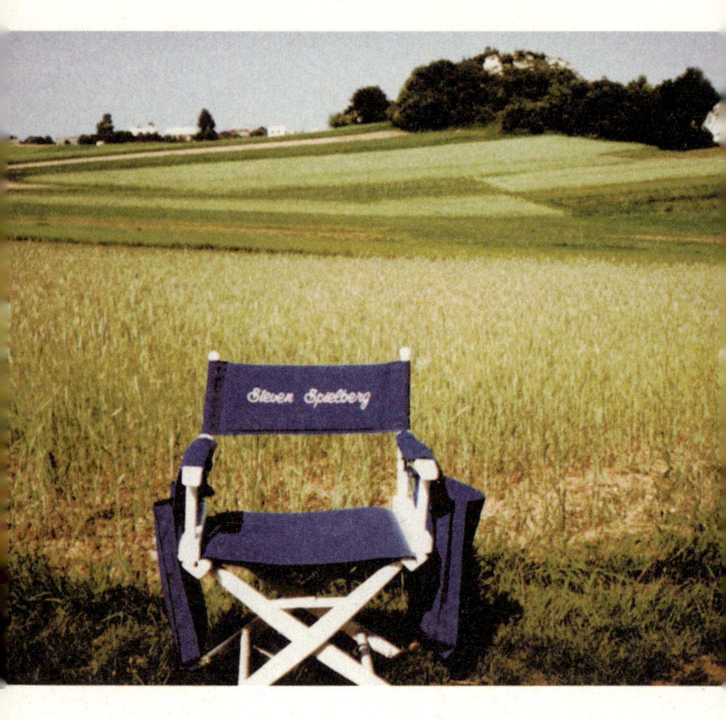

← ↑ OMER FAST, *Spielberg's List*, 2005
(details of video stills)

video retraces the last 20 minutes of the life of Argentine writer and leftist guerilla Roberto Walsh, who (according to the testimony of family, colleagues, and friends) was assassinated by government agents on March 25, 1977, after having criticized Jorge Rafael Videla's military dictatorship in an open letter. Unfolding in real time—the time it took for Walsh to walk from the Constitución Station to Calle Carlos Calvo, where he met his demise—the video allows the spectator to stand, as it were, in Walsh's shoes. The result is the uncanny experience of being—and *not* being—in Walsh's "place," of seeing and not seeing, knowing and not knowing what he underwent in his final moments of life.

In the Last 20 Minutes was created to provide a context for the collective's republication of Walsh's last work, *Un Oscuro Día de Justicia (A Dark Day of Justice)*—itself an example of the story's potential to document truths that cannot otherwise be told. An account of Walsh's boarding school years, the book describes schoolyard conflicts as an allegory of Argentina's political struggles. Originally published in 1973 in a period of relative freedom between two military dictatorships, the book was later banned. A copy was smuggled out of the country and made its way to a library in Amsterdam, where the collective is based. In the words of Missing Books, Walsh was a writer who "used fiction to tell the truth."[6] The same can be said of their imaginative recreation of the author's final moments: as it did with the other thousands of victims of Argentina's "dirty war," the government refused to publicly acknowledge Walsh's death, which officially never occurred.

The use of stories to negotiate—and even over-turn—distinctions between truth and fiction lies at the heart of *Spielberg's List*, Israeli artist Omer Fast's ambivalent meditation on the so-called Holocaust industry. Fast's two-screen installation features Polish extras from Steven Spielberg's 1993 blockbuster *Schindler's List*, the true, if melodramatically rendered, story of Oskar Schindler, a German businessman who saved the lives of more than a thousand Polish Jews during World War II by employing them in his factories. Echoing the interview format of the legendary Holocaust documentary *Shoah*, Fast's work likewise gives the extras the chance to tell their stories—not of the Holocaust (although some of the extras were children during the Nazi occupation) but of its recreation for the film. At times, their experiences as actors disturbingly echo those of the characters they played, as in the selection of "Jews" during the casting process. At other times, the two literally merge, as when an older man considers his participation in Spielberg's film against the backdrop of his childhood experience of one of its key episodes: the forced expulsion on October 28, 1942, of Krakow's Jews to Plaszów, a concentration camp located just outside the city's limits. In part a critique of the spectacularization of historical trauma in Hollywood films—the usurpation of an actual past by its cinematic representation—Fast's video avoids simplistic interpretation by also considering the very real way in which the extras' theatrical experiences, and their narration of them, influence their understanding of history. One sees this, for example, when a young Polish actor admits to himself for the first time that he had hoped to be cast as a German, not a Jew.

In his photo-essay *The Kant Walks*, Joachim Koester also takes up the legacy of World War II, albeit more obliquely, by retracing the ritualized daily walks of German Enlightenment philosopher Immanuel Kant through the streets of his hometown, Königsberg. Decimated by Allied bombs during the war—its historic center, cathedral, and medieval castle were all completely destroyed and never fully rebuilt—the once cosmopolitan Prussian city (or, better, its remains) was occupied in 1945 by the Soviet Union and renamed Kaliningrad after a founding member of the Bolshevik party. There are numerous conflicting accounts of Kant's preferred itinerary. Moreover, as Koester has pointed out, "one has to place two maps on top of each other, that of Königsberg and that of Kaliningrad, to find the locations today."[7] The perambulation that his photographs document was based on a map specially devised for the artist by a Kant scholar and Kaliningrad native. Still, despite the research involved, Koester's goal with *The Kant Walks* was not to accurately recover the philosopher's original route. Nor was it, as is the case with the Missing Books collective's *In the Last 20 Minutes*, to imaginatively recreate what the man who once walked a certain path might have seen. Indeed, the unbridgeable difference between what Kant witnessed on the 18th-century streets of Königsberg and what Koester encounters in 21st-century Kaliningrad is one of the points of his piece. (In one image, the viewer sees a small medieval fort stranded in an industrial quarter. Another presents the House of Soviets built on the former site of the Königsberg Castle. Now seemingly abandoned, it stands in the middle of an empty parking lot, a Stalinist-era ruin.) A "spatial story,"[8] to borrow a phrase from French sociologist Michel de

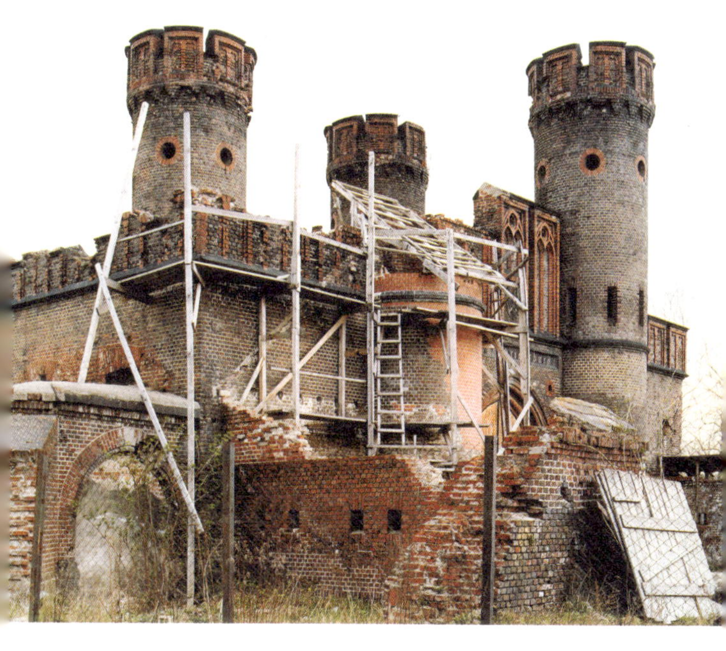

JOACHIM KOESTER, *#1*
(from the series *The Kant Walks*), 2003

JOACHIM KOESTER, *#3*
(from the series *The Kant Walks*), 2003 (detail) →

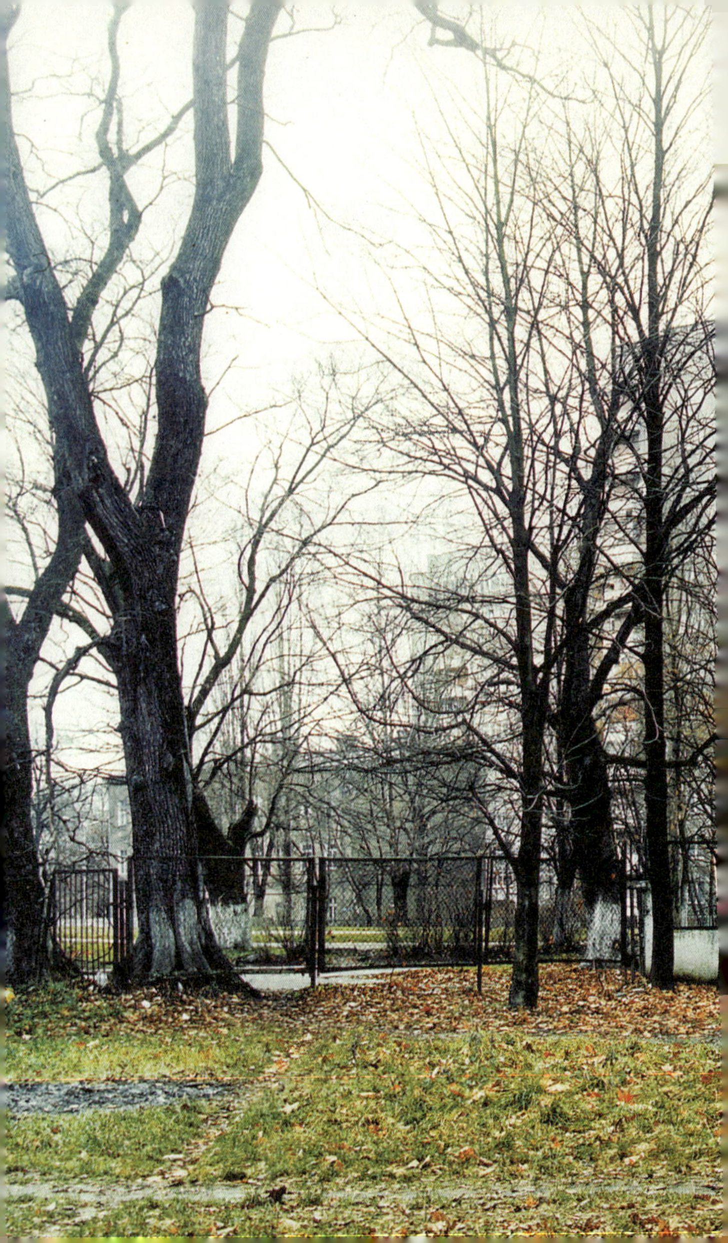

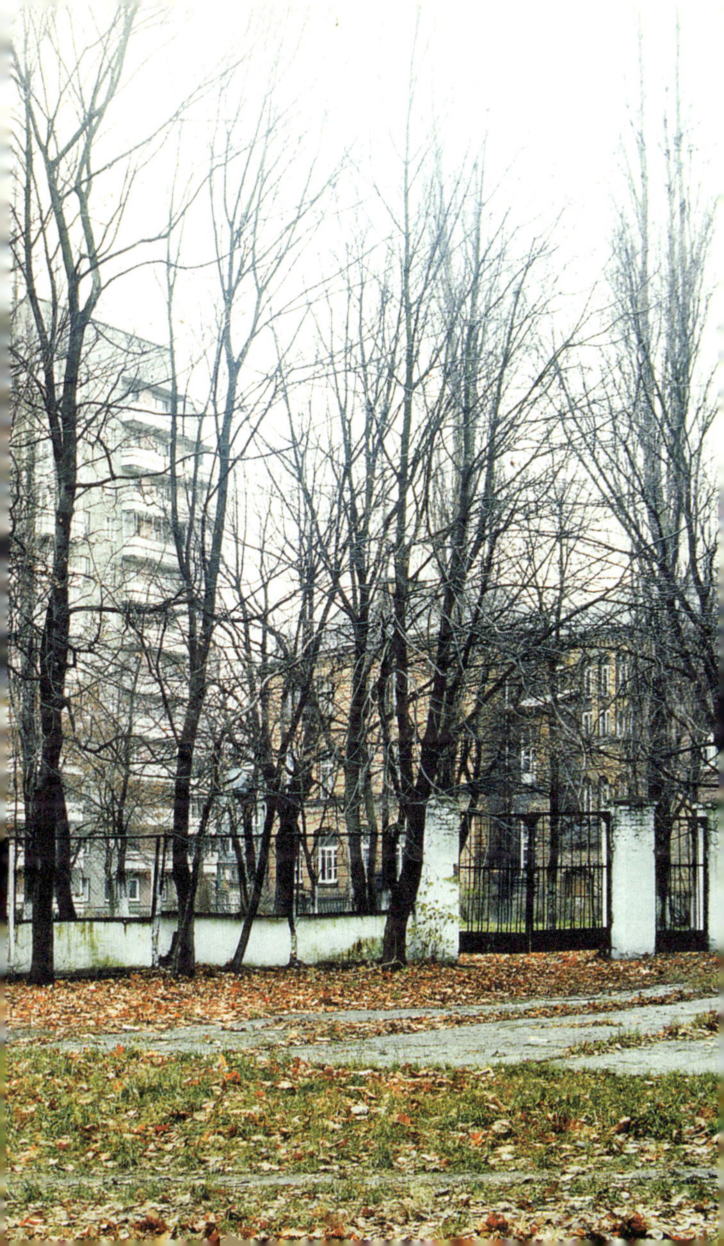

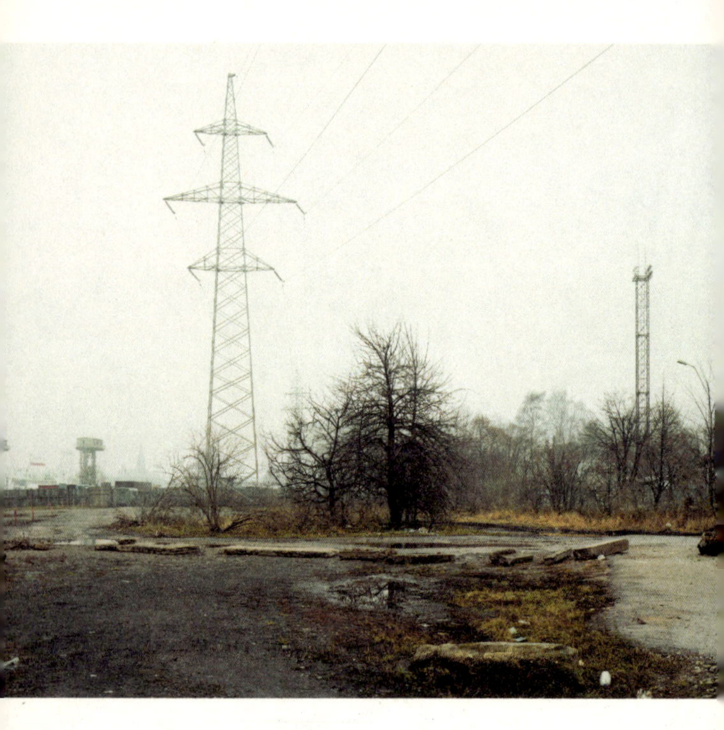

JOACHIM KOESTER, *#7*
(from the series *The Kant Walks*), 2003

Certeau, Koester's re-enactment is instead designed to reveal "hauntings from a war that shaped lives and destinies for generations to come, including my own."[9]

In the work of both Hito Steyerl and Liisa Roberts, it is less a place than a lost object that serves as the repository of a past accessed through stories—albeit an object with strong connotations of place. Steyerl's video, *Journal No. 1—An Artist's Impression,* takes as its subject the first Bosnian newsreel, which was shot in 1947 and destroyed in 1993 during the Bosnian civil war. For the piece, Steyerl invited two curators from the Sarajevo film museum to recount their memories of a scene from the newsreel—a literacy class offered to Muslim women as part of a general emancipation program under Tito—which she then commissioned a young Bosnian graphic artist to draw. The results of the two drawing sessions are presented side by side, highlighting the divergence between the curators' respective recollections. The discrepancy is in no way rectified by a third account offered by an old man who, as a boy, had attended the class documented in the newsreel with his grandmother. Steyerl further underscores the fallibility of human memory in a series of interviews with members of the staff of the film museum's storage facility and neighboring locals as to the newsreel's fate. (Some say it was stolen by Serbs and taken to Belgrade, others that it was evacuated to a nearby house that was subsequently bombed.) In the end, the newsreel cannot be recovered, either in the form of a physical object or as a definitive memory image. But as a platform for stories, it retains the power to organize an experience of national identity. Encompassing three generations, all touched in some way by the lost newsreel, Steyerl's work ends with the testimony of the young graphic artist describing his childhood experience of the war, fleeing Bosnia as a Muslim refugee.

For Liisa Roberts, a Finnish-American artist based in Helsinki, the "lost object" in question is, paradoxically, an existing building: the municipal library of the Russo-Finnish border town of Vyborg (formerly Viipuri), which, like Königsberg/Kaliningrad, changed both hands and names during World War II. One of the great works of modernist architect Alvar Aalto, the building was constructed in 1933, when Vyborg was under Finnish jurisdiction. Annexed by the Soviets in 1944, the city—along with its library—was heavily damaged during the war. Now, as Vyborg embarks on its current chapter as a Russian municipality on a newly open border, the Helsinki-based Committee for the Restoration of the Viipuri Library has initiated an at times problematically nostalgic campaign to restore Aalto's library to its original state. Given Aalto's insistence on the role of context and user, what, Roberts asked, "would it mean to recover the building's original condition, when the context and users for that building had so fundamentally changed?" Her response is *What's the Time in Vyborg?*, an ambitious multi-media project seeded by a creative writing workshop held in the library for a group of local teenagers—"the people," as Roberts notes, "who, coming of age after the end of the Cold War, will define the city's post-Soviet era." The workshop participants employed the panoramic view of Vyborg from the library's auditorium as a guiding metaphor, giving lyric and narrative form to the troubled past and imagined future of both library and city in stories they realized in a variety of media (film, installation, performance, broadcast spots on local TV). Powerfully harnessing the experiential possibilities engendered by the story form's ability to confound distinctions between fact and fiction, reality and representation, Roberts's work, in the artist's words, enabled the teenagers "to unfold the narrative of Aalto's library by writing within it their vision

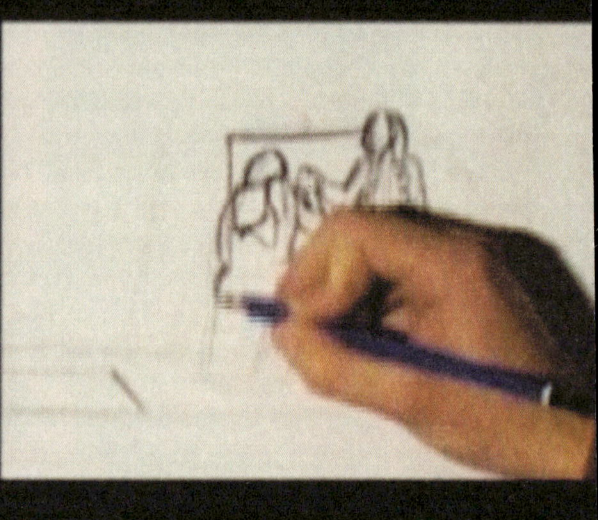

Maybe you have seen s
old movies.

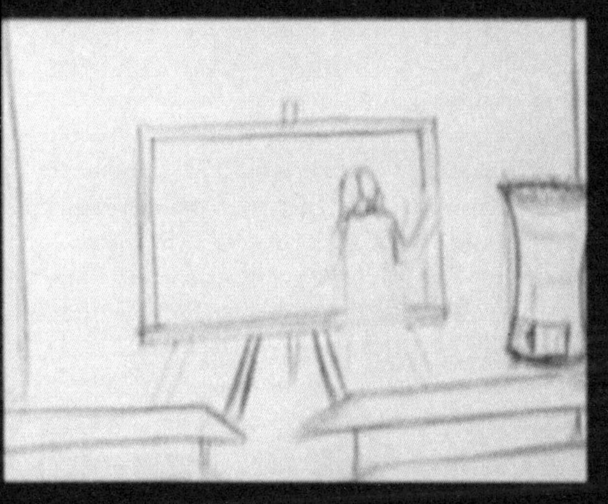

ething like it in

of the city of Vyborg, and then to live the unfolding narrative they'd helped to create."[10]

This notion of the story as something "lived" in the telling resonates powerfully with Jeremy Deller and Mike Figgis' *The Battle of Orgreave*, whose subject is the violent confrontation between striking miners and the British police that occurred on June 18, 1984, outside a coking plant in Orgreave, South Yorkshire. Wounding 123 and resulting in 93 arrests, the altercation was the climax of a three-month strike by the National Union of Mineworkers and signaled a decisive victory in the Thatcher government's bitterly fought neoliberal campaign to deregulate Britain's coal industry, described by some as a "civil war." Sixteen years after the fact, British artist Jeremy Deller restaged the event at its original location. Many who were part of the clash—both strikers and policemen—participated (although sometimes in reverse roles). They were joined by a group of seasoned amateur re-enactors versed in the recreation of historic military campaigns. Performed for local residents and the camera of renowned documentary filmmaker Mike Figgis, the event was elaborately staged, complete with police on horseback and in full riot gear. The video, *The Battle of Orgreave*—first broadcast on October 20,

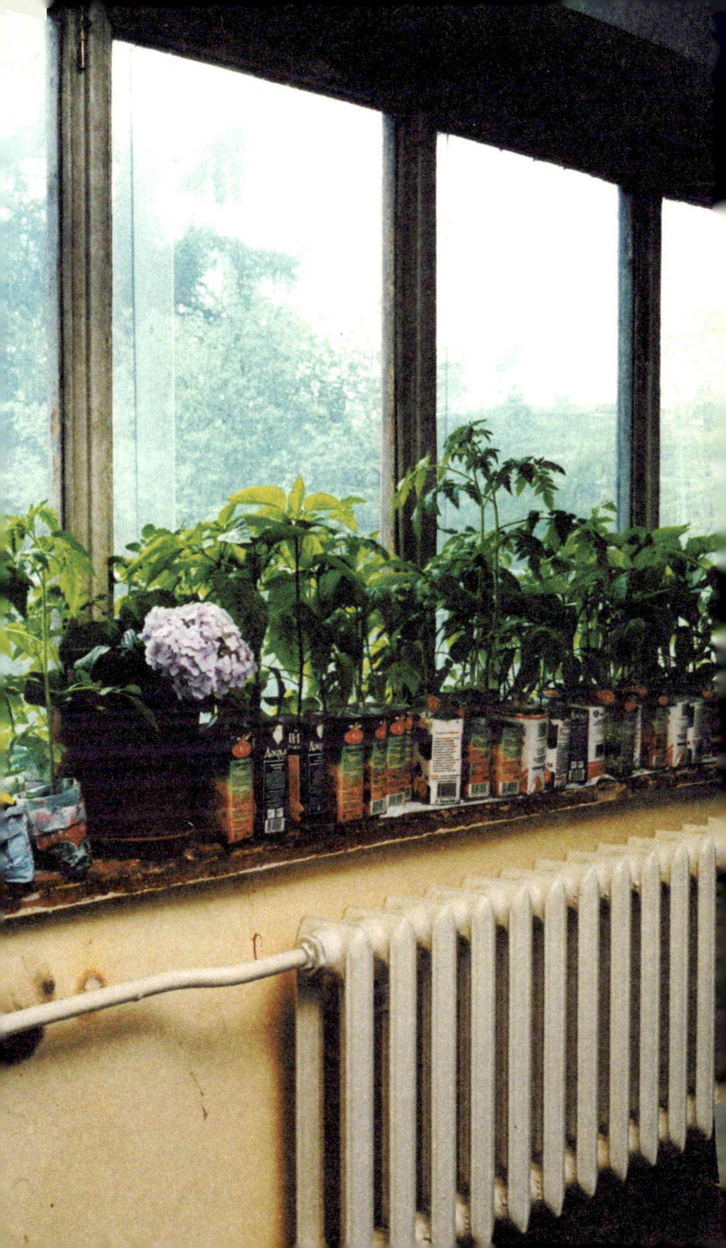

2002, on Britain's Channel 4—combines Figgis' footage of the reenactment, photographic stills of the original altercation, and interviews with the participants.

In this work, history emerges as an effect of storytelling on multiple levels. Its recreation of the past was plotted on the basis of stories told by those originally involved. Deller's restaging can itself be understood as a kind of performed story (one that points to the performative nature of the form as a whole.) The event, in turn, engendered new reflections on the past, recorded in Figgis' film. Finally, there is the "official" story put forth by the government and the BBC, which presented the miners not as wor-kers engaged in protest for job security but as rioters who, in Thatcher's own words, were Britain's "enemy within." It is this last story that Deller and Figgis' work both counters and redres-ses. It achieves this, in part, by affording the miners the chance to re-experience the event with dignity, by casting it as a story of a particular sort: one of the noble, legendary battles that make up the canon of historical reenactment.

The Meaning of Form

As Benjamin noted, stories exist to be told.

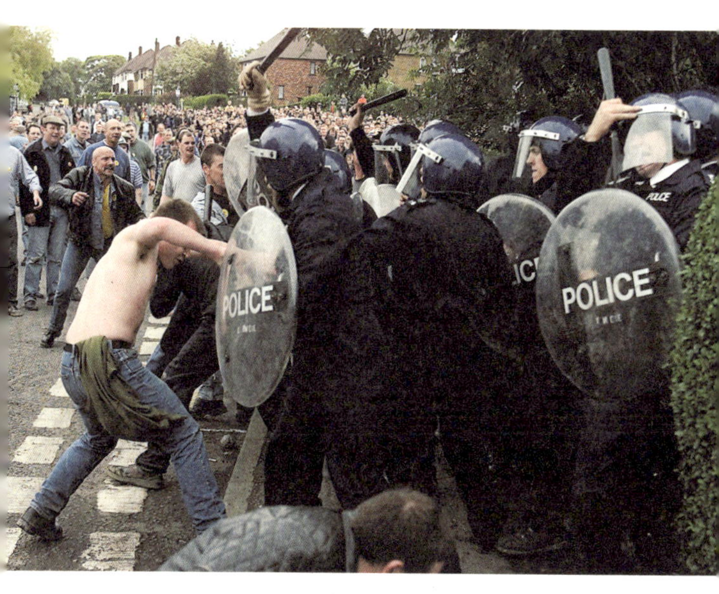

← ← ← ← HITO STEYERL, *Journal No. 1—An Artist's Impression*, 2007 (video still)

← LIISA ROBERTS, *Alvar Aalto Vyborg Library*, March 2001 (research photograph)

JEREMY DELLER AND MIKE FIGGIS, *The Battle of Orgreave*, 2002 (production stills) ↑ →

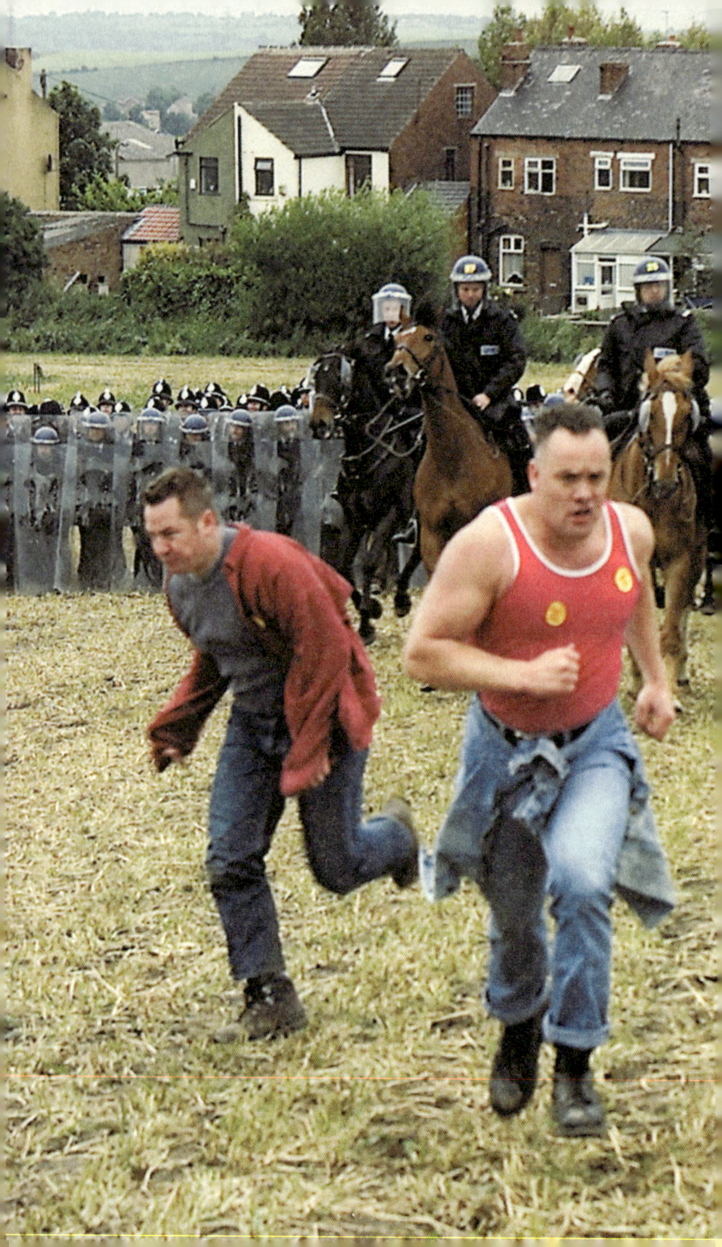

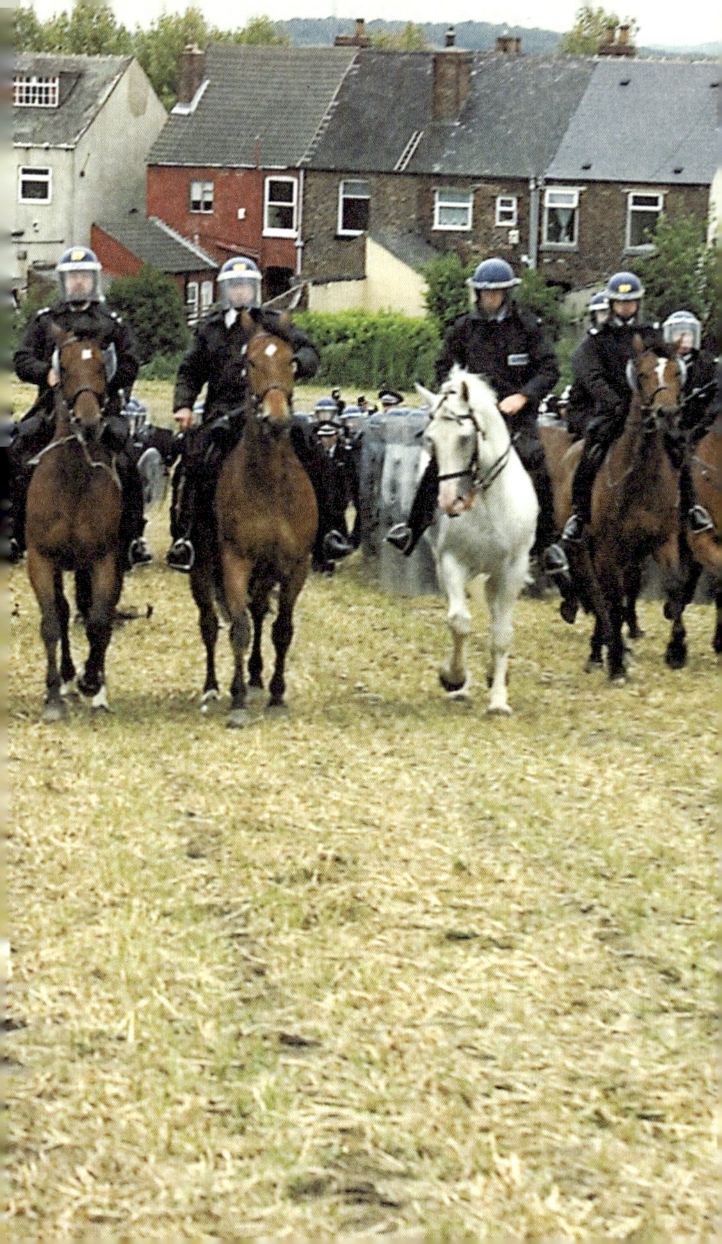

Benjamin further described the mode through which that communication occurs as "an artisan form."[11] That is to say, unlike information or news reports, which aspire to objectivity, stories are manifestly *made*. They come from someone and the form they assume means something. In Adrian Paci's 1997 video *Albanian Stories*, the form of choice is the fairytale, specifically as employed by the artist's three-year-old daughter Jolanda. Shortly after leaving Albania for Italy following the economic collapse and resulting riots of 1997, Paci discovered his daughter playing with her dolls while reciting improvised fairytales about the family's exodus. The video features Jolanda recounting these stories, in which folkloric characters, such as a cow, cock, and cat, encounter "dark forces" and big flames before being saved by "international forces." As Paci's daughter carefully repeats her tales with notable variation ("once upon a time there was a cow [...] and here is the end of the story [...] once upon a time there was a cock and a cat [...]"), we see her sustained effort to come to terms with a reality that often overreaches her own capacity for expression. Frequent pauses and nonsensical phrases interrupt the narrative flow even as Jolanda remains calm, using the modulations of her voice and elaborate hand gestures to craft a compelling tale.

This is her moment, her story; indeed, in filming his daughter's private musings, Paci has granted her an audience, thus fulfilling storytelling's essential public function. As Tolkien observed, fantasy is not so much distinct from reality as parallel to it.[12] Alternative worlds provide the necessary distance to make sense of complicated real-world events. Perhaps this is why fairytales cross cultural and national borders. Paci's daughter chooses the fairytale form because it is familiar, a template into which she can easily insert her own traumatic circumstances. In presenting her efforts to us, Paci demonstrates the form's accessibility, delivering a testament to the particularity and universality of conflict and our attempts to comprehend it.

The fairytale genre also structures Cao Fei's *Whose Utopia*, a video the artist made in collaboration with workers at a Guangdong province lightbulb factory in 2006. For this piece, Fei asked the Chinese workers to enact their ideal occupation. The result is a three-part video set in the factory that is divided, much like a traditional story, into distinct chapters: "Imagination of Product," "Factory Fairytale," and "My Future is not a Dream." An initial, tightly framed focus on the modernist efficiency of machines at work (no people are seen until midway through the

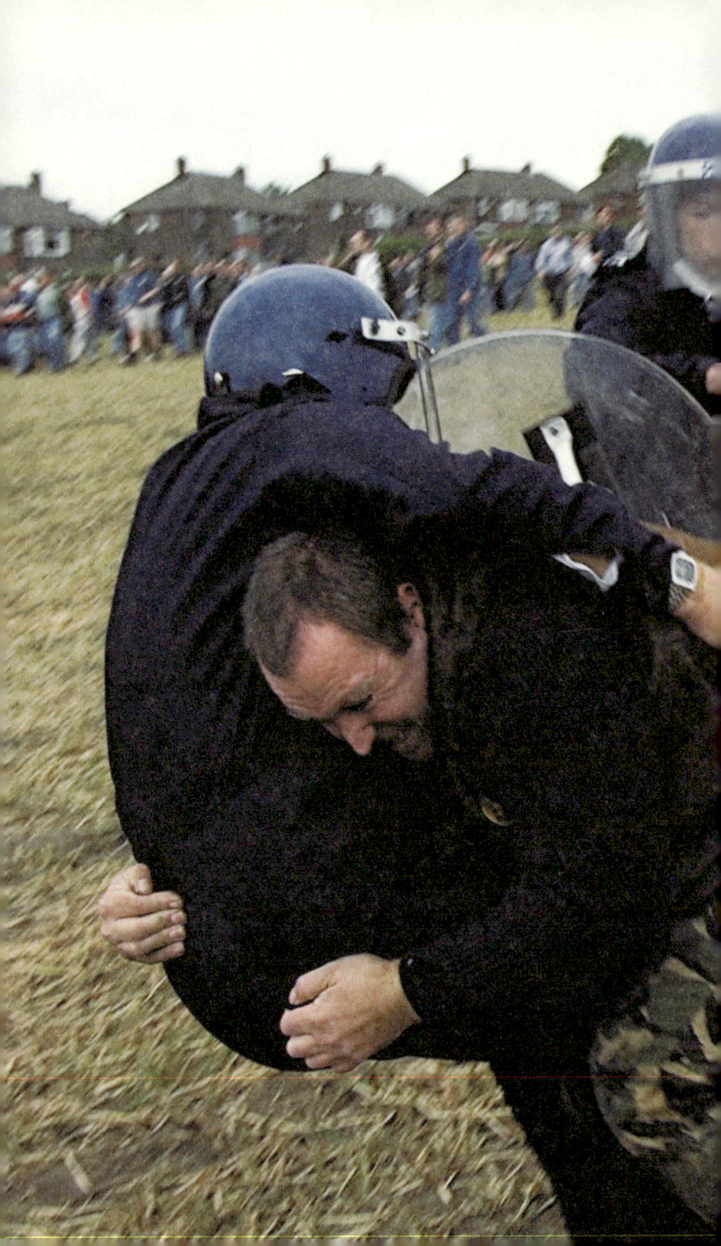

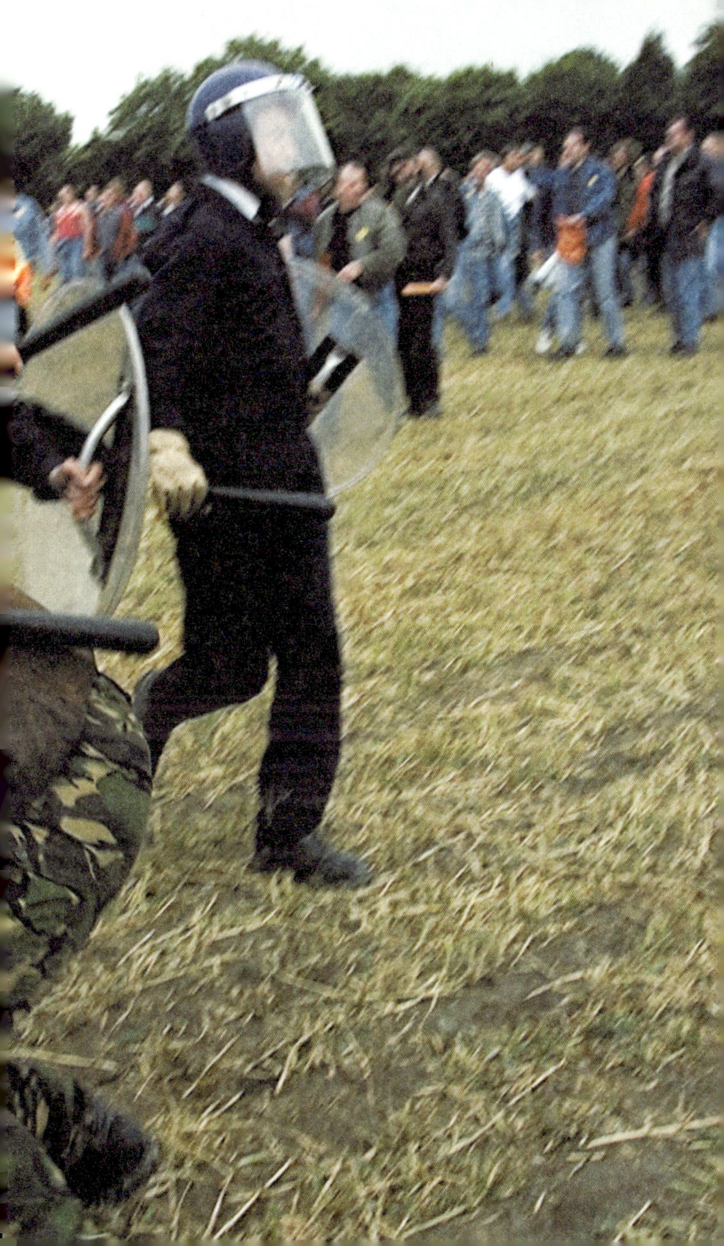

first segment), gives way in the second and third chapters to the factory workers' imaginative enactments of their chosen personas. Dressed as ballerinas, traditional Chinese dancers, or rock musicians complete with band t-shirts and guitars, the "actors" move in and out of the machines to an emotionally stirring score composed by a local rock band. That their personas are expressed in each case through music or dance underscores the contrast between the alienation of factory production and the intimacy of their self-made identities. Much as in *Albanian Stories*, it would seem that these stories are what allow their authors to keep going.

Storytelling operates on two registers in *Whose Utopia*. First, there are the factory workers' songs and pantomimes, however obscure their delivery. But there is also the story of the film itself: the story of Chinese industry or, better yet, of a certain kind of life in capitalist China. Fei gives this story a human face, revealing the multiple individual narratives with which it is composed. In doing so, she takes pains to assert the manufactured nature of her endeavor—this is, after all, a film in three acts—but this overt construction does not make Fei's endeavor any less true. Indeed, the video's lyrical, fableistic tone enables her to capture the potency of her

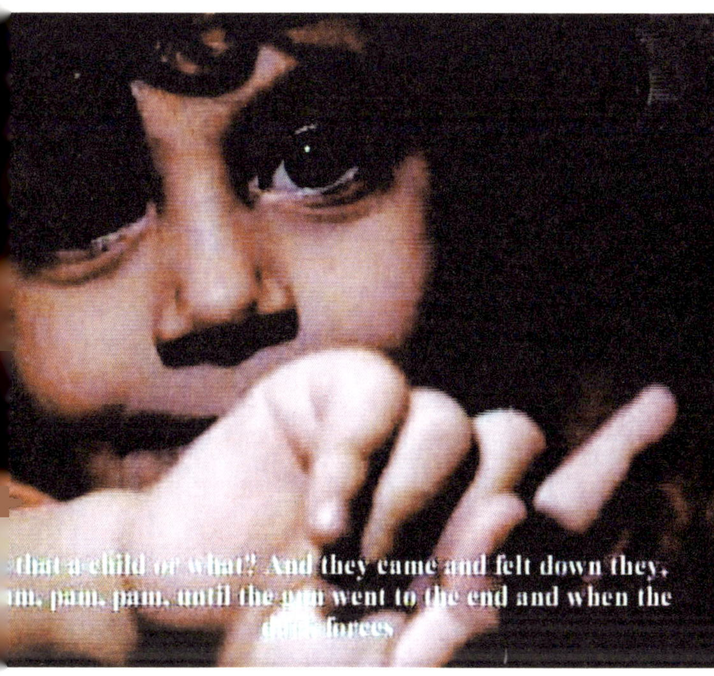

← ← ← JEREMY DELLER AND MIKE FIGGIS, *The Battle of Orgreave*, 2002 (production still)

ADRIAN PACI, *Albanian Stories*, 1997 (video still)

subjects' aspirations without presuming to encompass their reality.

As Fei's title indicates, it is humanity's ever elusive desires that are, more than anything else, her subject. Ryan Gander is equally preoccupied with unrealized dreams—in his case, with the evanescent goals of architectural modernism. The sculpture *As Time Elapsed* takes as its point of departure the 2005 children's book *The Boy Who Always Looked Up*, written and illustrated by Gander. More specifically, the colorful floating wall sculpture is made out of the book (and 31 dummy copies), which tells the story of the death of architect Ernö Goldfinger—the creator of the infamous Trellick Tower built in Notting Hill in 1973—as seen through the eyes of a fictional boy named Tom, who lives in the shadow of Goldfinger's 32-story building. Conceived as an ideal public housing structure, the project went badly awry; for years, the building was plagued by crime and general disrepair. The book itself is a poignant tale of dashed hopes sustained by the boy's persistent aspiration, while the elusive floating sculpture compliments the sense of impossible wonder at the story's core. Just as the fairytale form suits Paci and Fei, so too does the children's book genre (with its emphasis on goodness of heart and belief in the face of

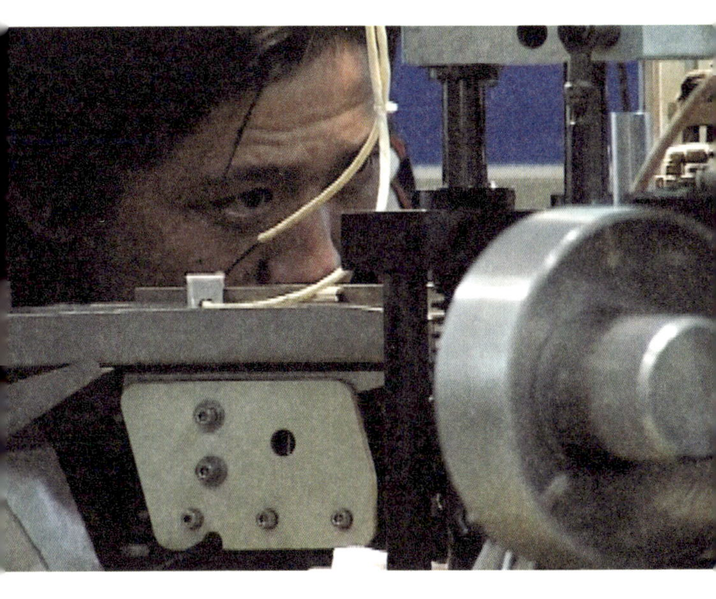

CAO FEI, *Whose Utopia*, 2006 (video still)

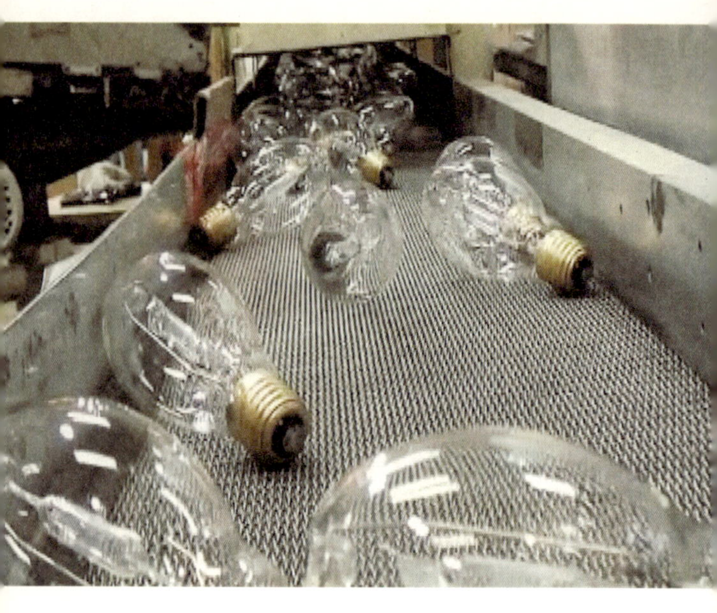

CAO FEI, *Whose Utopia*, 2006 (video stills) ↑ → →

adversity) suit Gander's historical subject. If history cannot be corrected, Gander's project suggests, at least its motivations can be preserved. Gander's book and sculpture lends substance to the dreams that animated the recent past, dreams that are as tenuous as the forms within which he delivers them. Through the mode of the children's story and art object—itself a kind of fiction—Gander respects and recreates their utopian vision. His magical sculpture, placed high up on the wall, allows the viewer to re-experience Tom's sensation of gazing up at Trellick Tower even as it ensures that we recall our own position here and now.

It is not incidental that Gander's piece is about a failed construction project. Mounir Fatmi's work also takes building as its theme. The sculptural installation *Save Manhattan 02*, assembles videotapes—a once ubiquitous, now obsolete form of communication—on a table to recreate the New York skyline pre-9/11, two stacks of cassettes standing in for the ill-fated Twin Towers. The tape is pulled out in places, spilling over the side of the table in a chaotic black stream. On first look, Fatmi's gesture seems to indicate an act of destruction—it is as though the recorded histories contained in the outdated cassette tapes are no longer

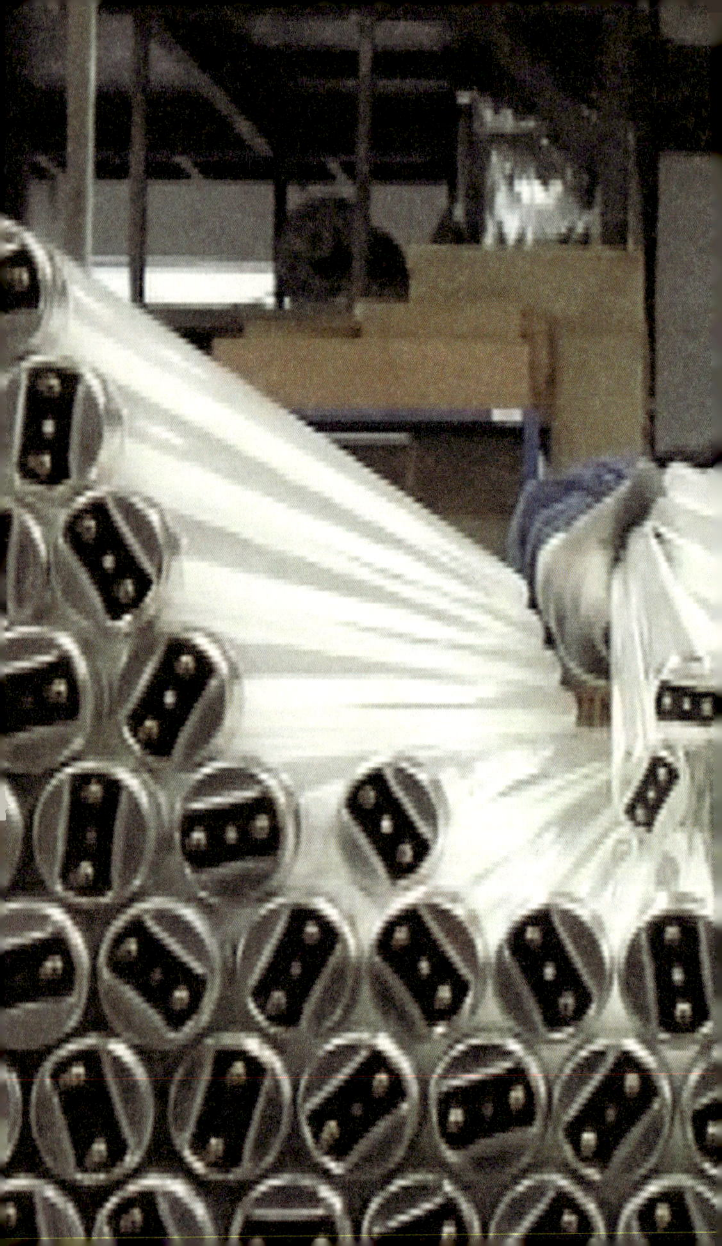

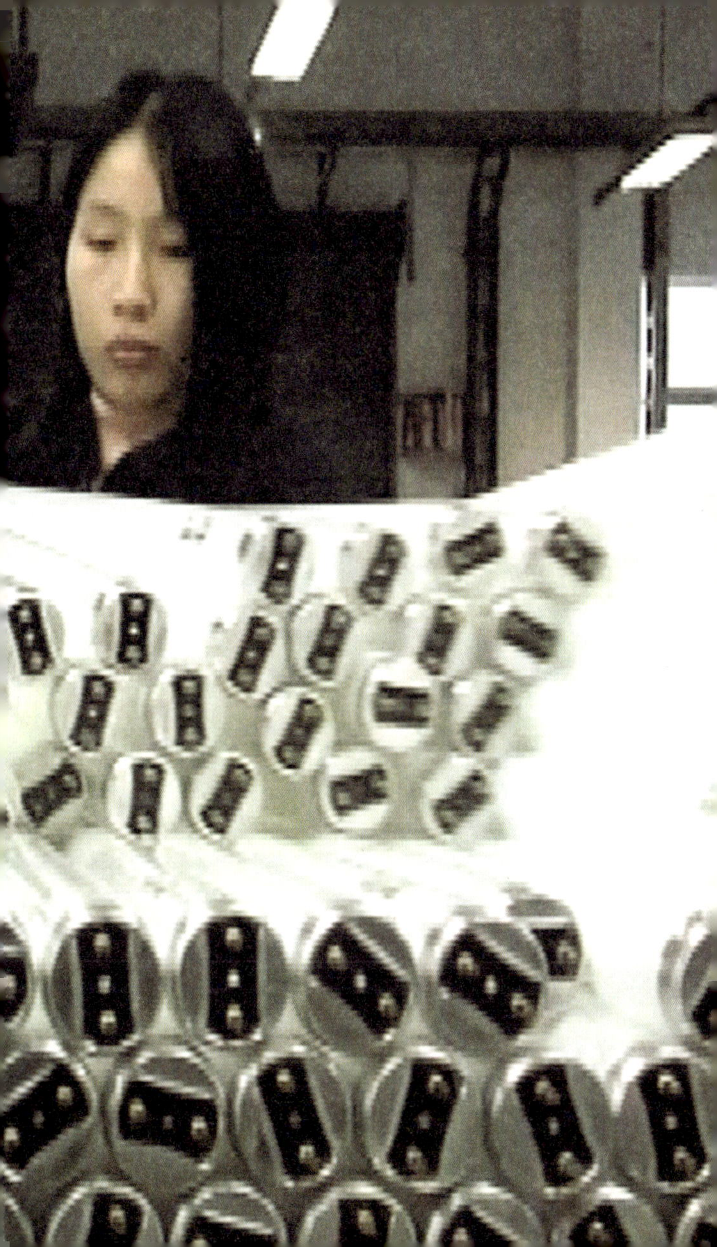

serviceable, reading instead as a tangled sculptural mass. And yet, their literal imbrication also indicates a desperate need to sort through and make sense of what happened. According to Fatmi, while political crises cast doubt on the validity of traditional institutions like religion and statehood, they also necessitate new commitments, new attempts at building. In *Save Manhattan 02*, the cassettes stand their ground against their contents' downward pull in a fragile configuration that, model-like, stands somewhere between past and future. Are we meant to restore the recorded stories to their discreet containers or instead to reconfigure them in new stories that take into account the temporary nature of all attempts at coming to terms with history?

Fatmi has made several different versions of *Save Manhattan*. In one sculpture, the videocassettes stand unmolested on the floor. Other sculptures replace the videotapes with fiction and nonfiction books, with the Koran occupying the place of the Twin Towers. Fatmi has tailored this piece to the country in which the work is shown. Hence, German books about 9/11 when the work is exhibited in Germany; French books in France; and the Koran, in each case, in translation. The ramifications of the events of

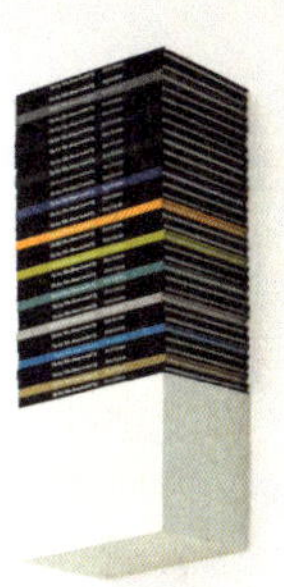

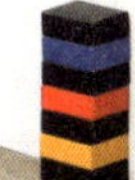

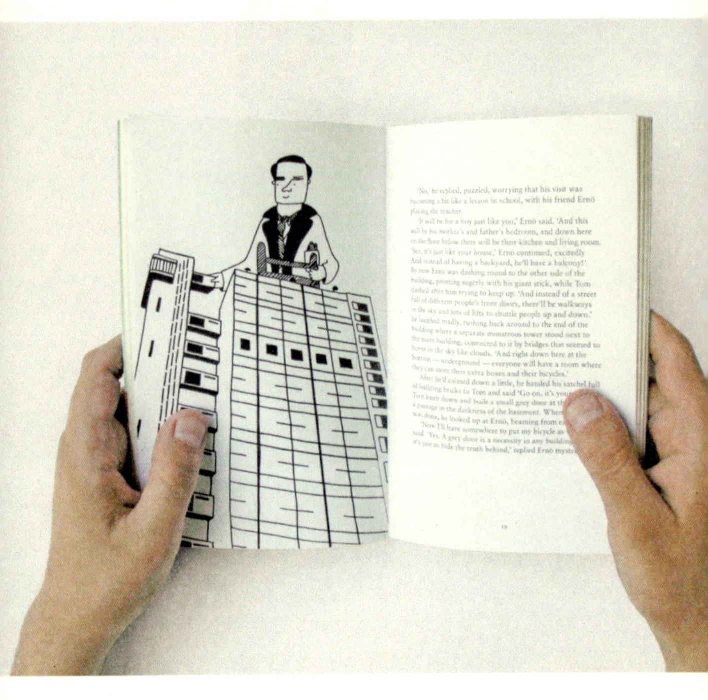

← RYAN GANDER, *As Time Elapsed*, 2005
↑ RYAN GANDER, detail of the book *The Boy Who Always Looked Up*, 2005

50

September 11, 2001, have reached far beyond America's borders and, in its many incarnations, Fatmi's work captures the intersection between the local and the global that defines today's world. *Save Manhattan* brings together different elements—nationally specific books versus the seemingly universal, yet still indecipherable videotapes—in an evolving testament to the necessity of reconfiguration. Stories beget stories (forms beget forms) and Fatmi's sculpture illustrates this accumulation and diversity.

Modes of Reception

To recognize that the form a narrative assumes impacts the story told is to acknowledge that stories change in the telling. As noted, stories generate stories just as any individual narrator is in turn influenced by the events he or she has seen, heard about, or experienced. This is the basic premise behind Lamia Joreige's *Objects of War*, an ongoing video project begun in 1999 and consisting of testimonials about the Lebanese civil war, a conflict that persisted throughout the artist's formative years, from 1975 to 1990. For each video, Joreige asked Lebanese residents of varying ages to select a personal object that for them best reflects their experience of the war. Following one after the next, the highly

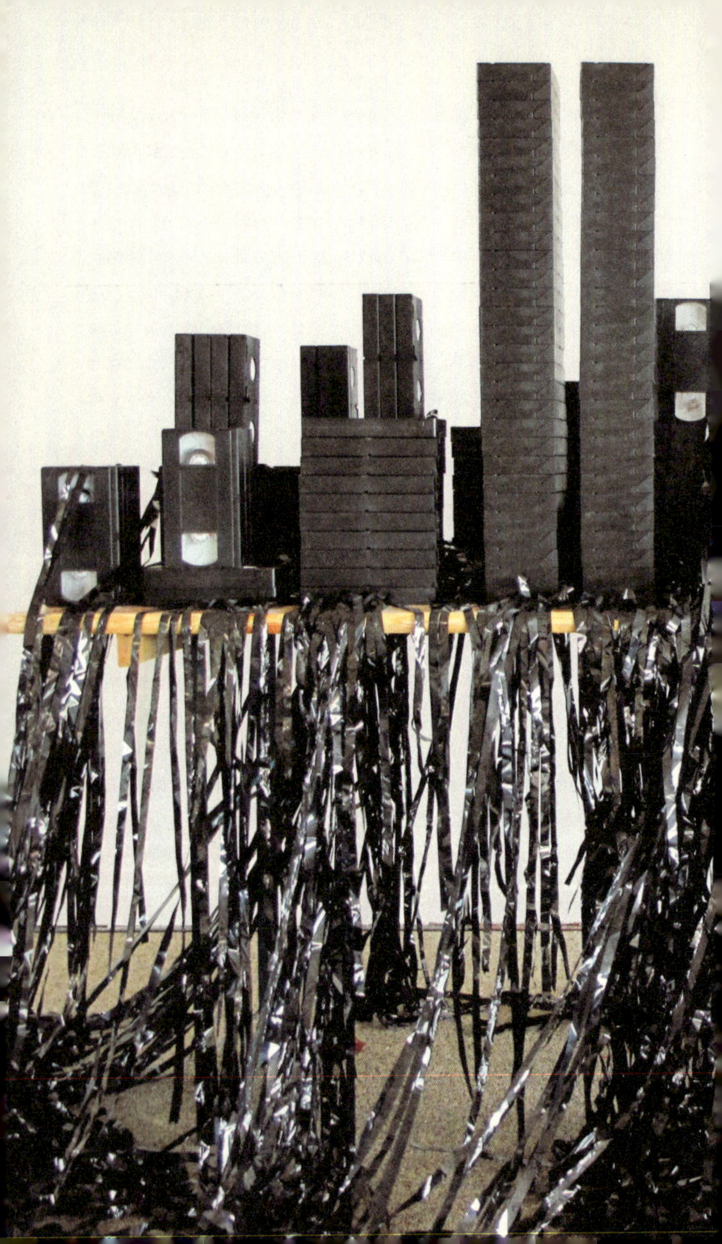

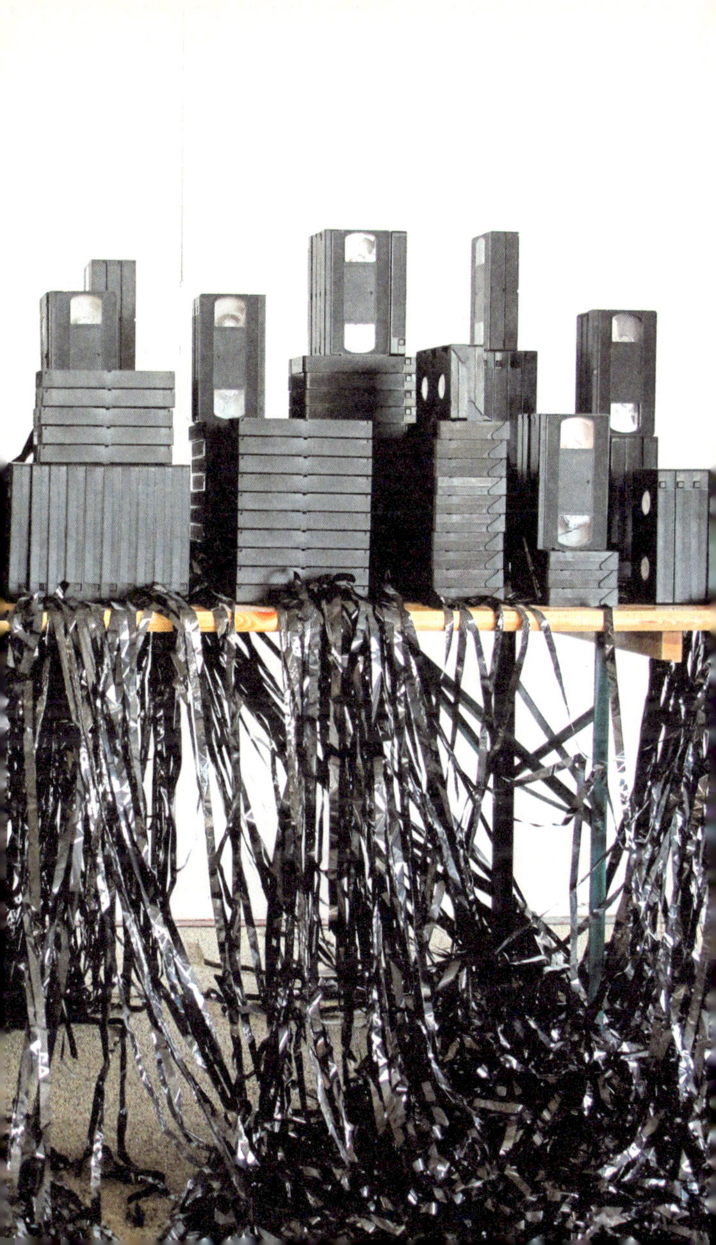

varied testimonies expose the emotional and psychological reality behind the war's official history. The presentation of two or more videos, commonly installed side by side, affirm the possibility of shared experience while denying any totalized representation of history.

Joreige's piece also concerns the way in which stories themselves influence history, affecting our actions and decisions. More than anything else, *Objects of War* is about dialogue: the tales passed down from father to son, the relationship between past and future selves, the secrets confessed by emotionally exposed subjects. In one segment, a young man shows a drawing of planes by his five-year-old son (*Objects of War n° 4* is the first video in which Joreige's subjects reflect on recent events like the 2006 Israeli invasion) explaining that he is in the same position vis-à-vis his son as his parents were with respect to him 20 years ago. Just as his understanding of the civil war depended on what his parents did and did not tell him, so too is his child's awareness of recent events informed by the man's own selective narrative. Context filters experience. In much the same way, the chosen objects allow the interviewees to concentrate their overwhelming sensations. This is true for the artist herself, who has explained that it was only after making the first

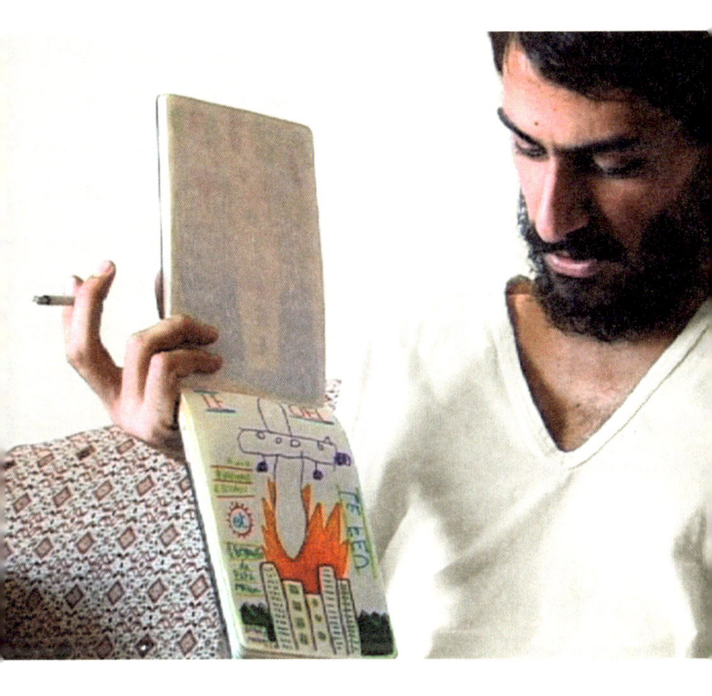

← ← MOUNIR FATMI, *Save Manhattan 02*, 2009

LAMIA JOREIGE, *Objects of War n° 4*, 2006 (video still)

three videos—her own "objects" of war—that she had the courage to come to terms with her feelings about the past and begin to face the present. Dialogue between generations is also fundamental to Michael Rakowitz's *Return*, another long-term project that originated in 2006, when the artist resurrected his Iraqi-Jewish grandfather's import-export business in order to bring Iraqi dates to the US for the first time in 25 years. For *The Storyteller*, Rakowitz's installation recalls the store in Brooklyn that he temporarily occupied, complete with wall panels, date products, objects involved in transport, as well as emails, blog reports, and a recent video detailing his experience making the piece and his conversations with the people involved. Although the original project had practical goals, the store was above all a place of communicative exchange. The dates did not arrive until just a few weeks before the store was scheduled to close, and yet the piece remains effective as a way of bringing a situation into public view—with the dates (much like Joreige's objects of war) serving as a concrete locus around which discussion accumulated. In its current incarnation, the narrative takes place on multiple levels. There is a history of dates, which informs us, via the Koran, that Mary took shelter under a date palm during Jesus's birth and consumed its leaves

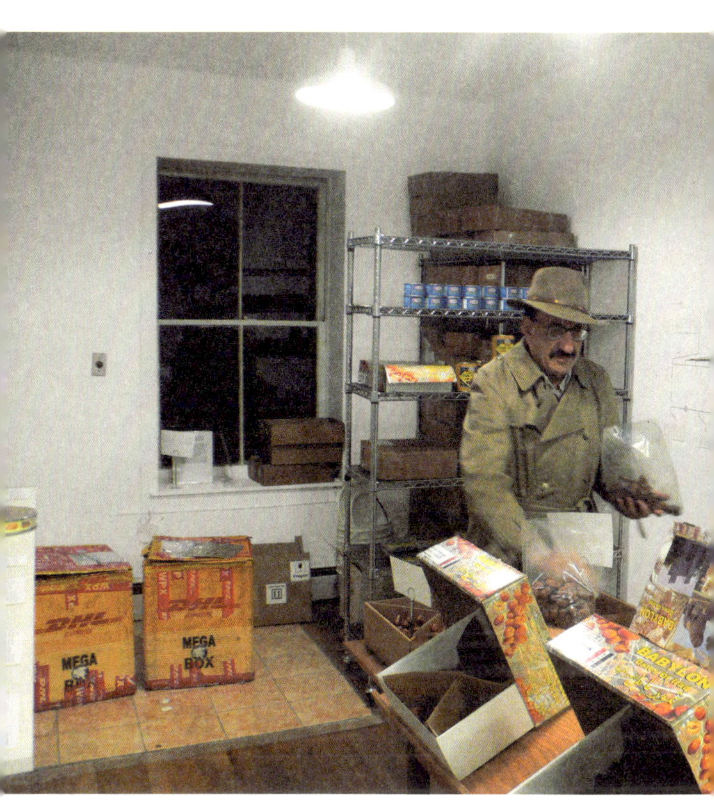

MICHAEL RAKOWITZ, *Return (Brooklyn)*, 2006
(installation view at Davisons & Co. import/export company,
Brooklyn, New York)

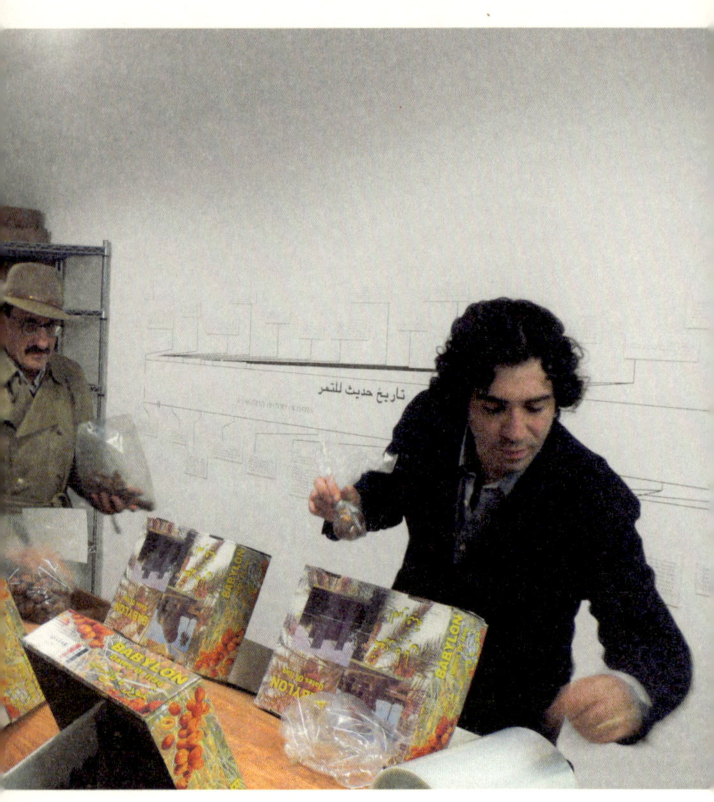

MICHAEL RAKOWITZ, *Return (Brooklyn)*, 2006
(installation view at Davisons & Co. import/export company,
Brooklyn, New York)

to ease her labor pains. There are the individual stories, such as that of Hanna Ali of East Petersberg, Pennsylvania, whose niece was orphaned in Iraq by Islamic extremists. And there is Rakowitz's own narrative as he considers in the blog and video what the project means and will continue to mean if he is able to resurrect it in Chicago as he plans: how it has affected the people involved, what it says about the war in Iraq, and, above all, what it means to him and his personal history. Rakowitz's artistic intervention is ultimately symbolic. As he himself acknowledges, it cannot fundamentally alter history. What it does provide is a space for reflection.

Dissatisfied with the media coverage of the war in Iraq, American artist Steve Mumford sought a similar space when he traveled in 2003 to the war-torn country armed with his sketchpad. Over the course of numerous, ongoing trips, Mumford has produced a series of lyrical water-colors and ink drawings that depict his exper-ience of daily life in and around Baghdad, including images of soldiers, oil fields, and mass graves, as well as encounters with Iraqi artists, local workers, and the serene countryside. The quiet concentration necessitated by his chosen medium might have made for a largely private experience. And yet it was precisely the personal

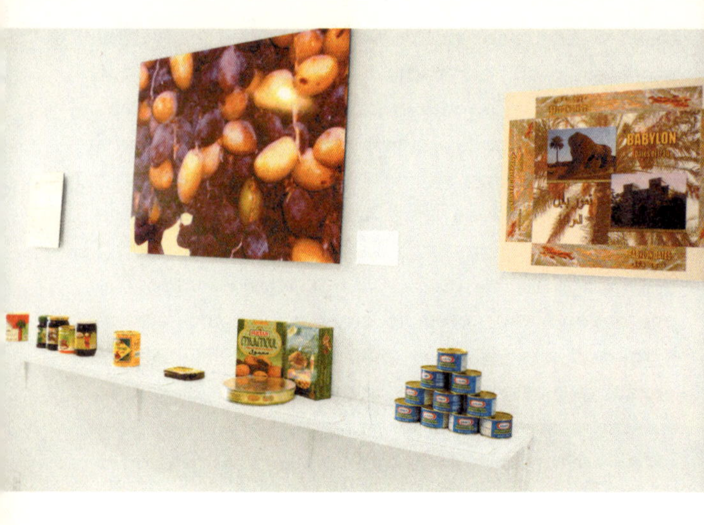

MICHAEL RAKOWITZ, *Return (Brooklyn)*, 2006
(installation view at Davisons & Co. import/export company,
Brooklyn, New York)

STEVE MUMFORD, *13A3, John, a contractor, giving a
firearms class to Iraqi police in Khalis, July, 2004. The
Iraqis had to be convinced to replace the rifle stocks on
their AKs for better aiming, although it didn't look as cool.*
(from the series *Iraq, 2003–2005*), 2004 (detail) → →

time and dedication required that enabled Mumford to respond to the intricacies of life in Iraq in a way that television reporting could not. As the artist has observed, "if photojournalism captures a decisive moment, making a drawing is more about lingering with a place and editing the scene in a wholly subjective way. It's never com-prehensive of the visual facts, which are filtered through one's senses, selected, exaggerated, or left out over the hour or so that it takes to make a drawing. As the drawing evolves, the scene changes, offering new possibilities. For me, the act of drawing slowed down the war, recording the spaces in between the bombs."[13]

Drawing is in this sense a form of reception. It responds to the changing landscape. In Mumford's case, the mere fact of choosing an idiosyncratic medium generated interest. He has recounted how, seeing him with his sketchpad, people came over to meet him, eager to share their stories. These conversations in turn influenced the final images in a never-ending cycle. Much like Rakowitz's multi-layered pro-ject, the drawings are only a small portion of what might be considered Mumford's work in Iraq. His time there has also yielded blog reports and a book, entitled *Baghdad Journal*, in which Mumford paired the drawings with anecdotes

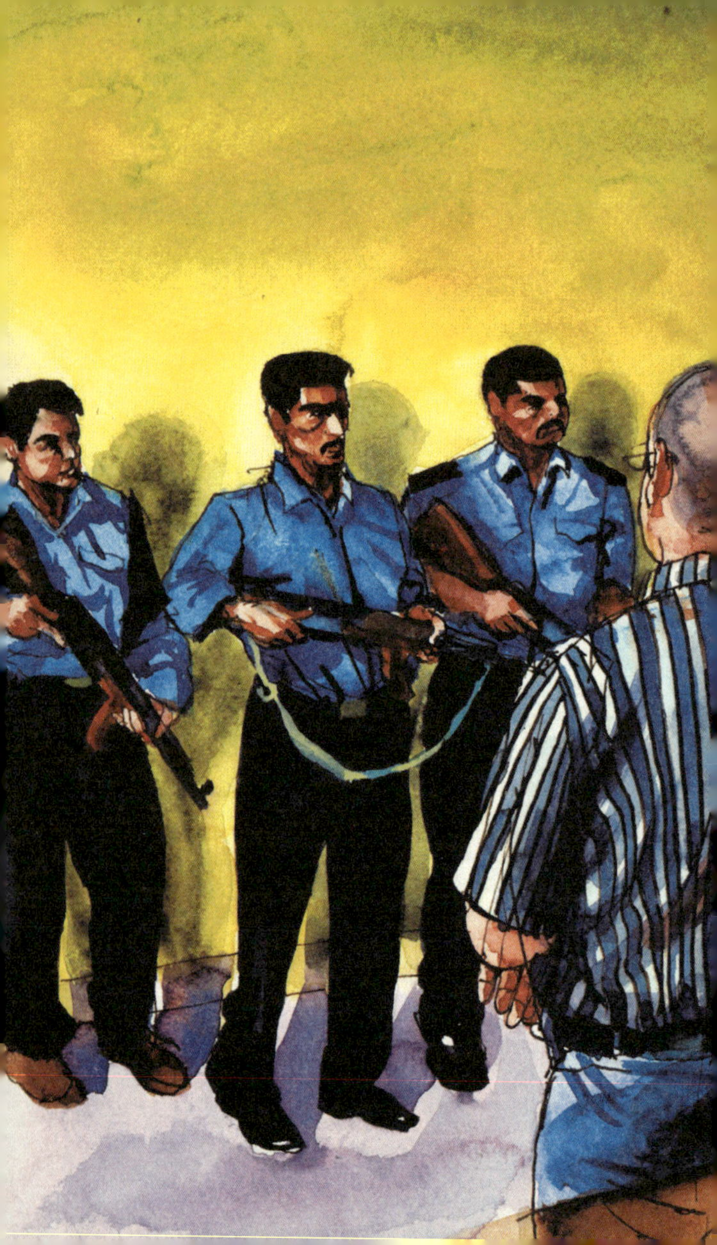

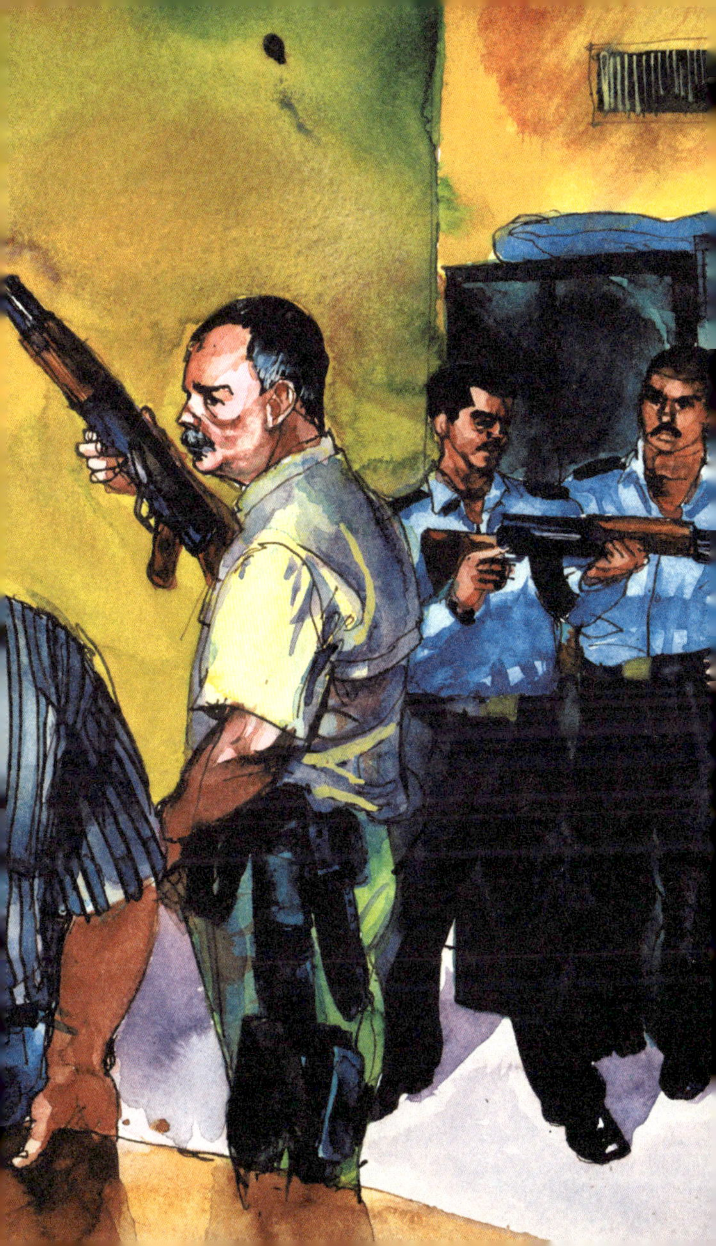

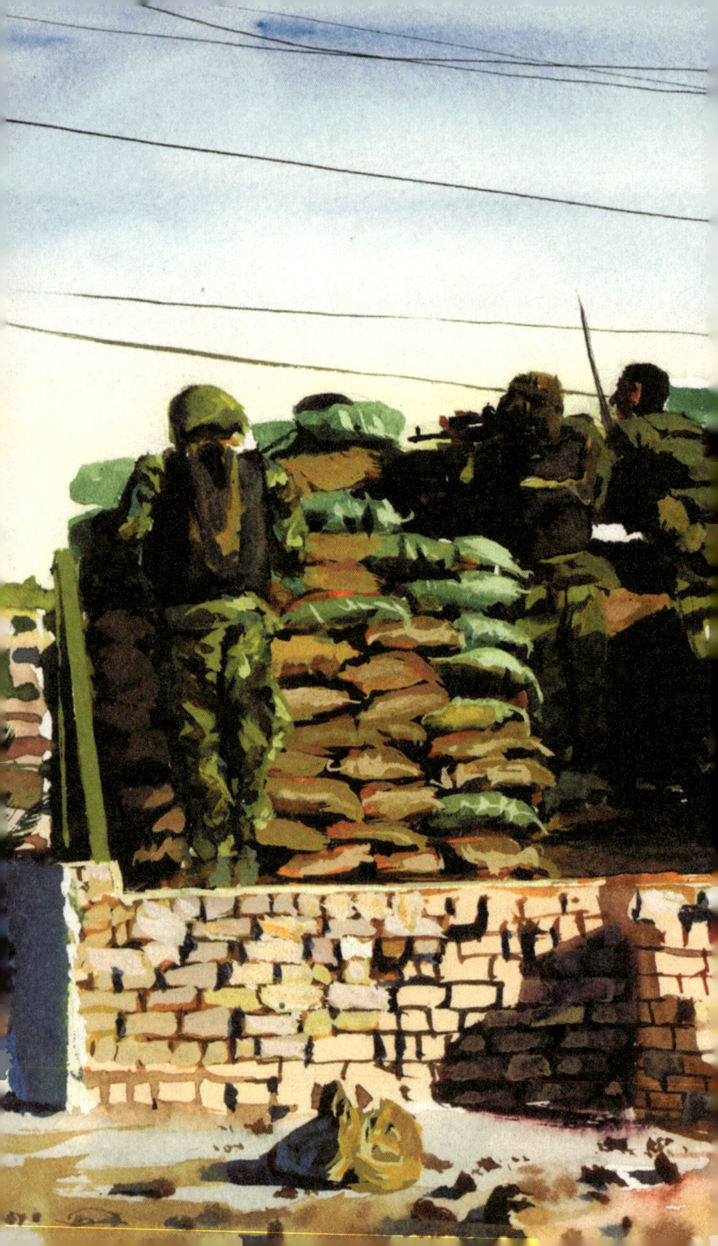

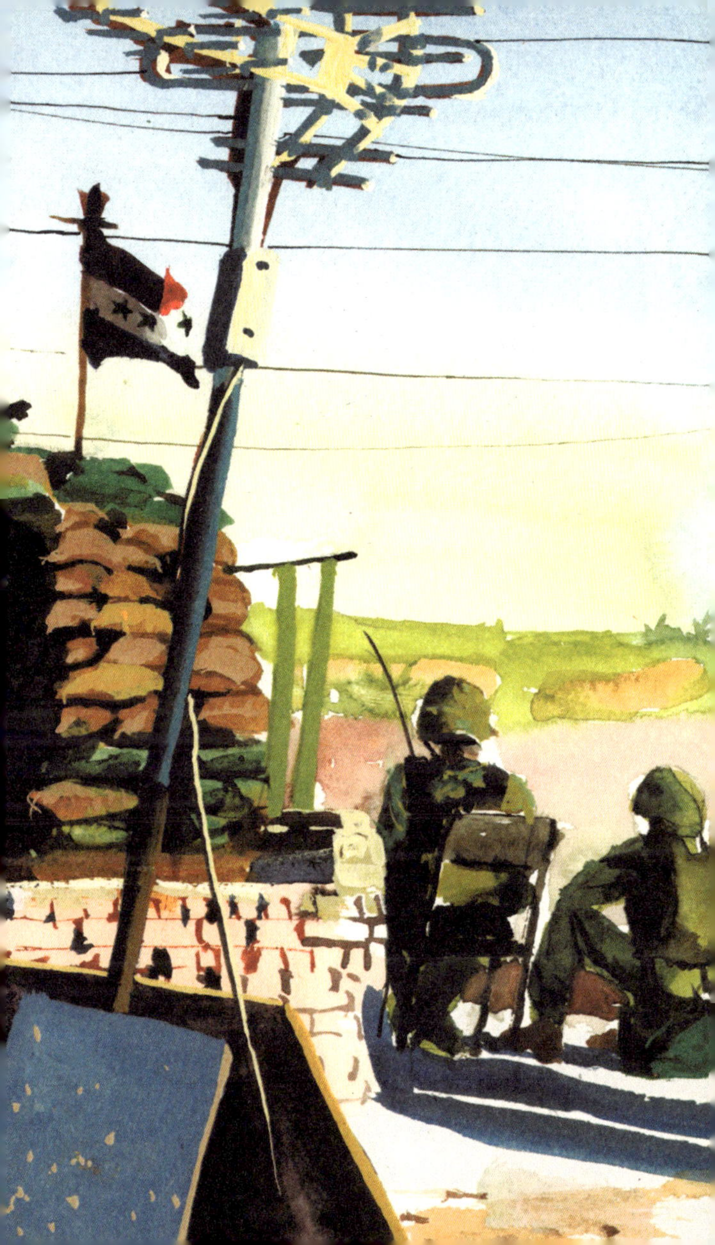

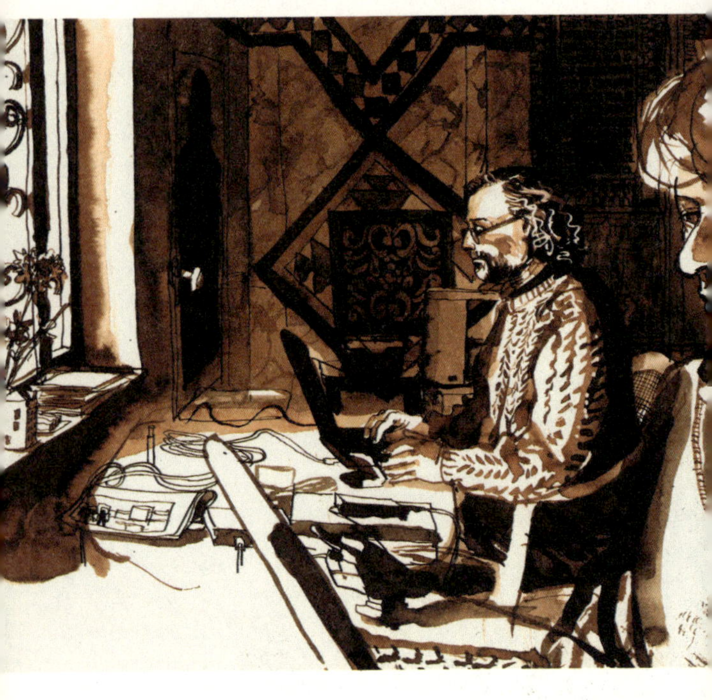

STEVE MUMFORD, *9A6, Jean-Claude Chapon and Paul Garwood, reporters at FOB Iron Horse, Tikrit, March, 2004. (from the series Iraq, 2003–2005), 2004*

← STEVE MUMFORD, *13B4, Georgian (Republic of Georgia) snipers on the Hibhib police station roof watching a bomb discovered on the street being rigged to be "blown in place" by an EOD squad. (from the series Iraq, 2003–2005), 2004 (detail)* from and about the people he met there, now his friends and companions. Interestingly, Mumford was motivated to travel to Iraq because of his powerful impressions of the Vietnam War, which he learned about as a child through pictures and second-hand accounts. In going to Iraq, Mumford experienced war first hand, creating an intimate vision that will undoubtedly impel future investigations and future stories.

Perhaps we should conclude by saying that Walter Benjamin was wrong. Or at least, if we consider the artists discussed, it would seem that, far from vanishing, storytelling is once again coming into view. Its re-emergence, this exhibition suggests, is best understood within the framework of a broader documentary impulse in contemporary art: an urgent need to bear witness to our complex world. Through recourse to the story, the artists surveyed here not only accomplish that task but do so in a way that fundamentally expands our understanding of what documentary "truth" might be: the story is a document of a different sort—one whose focus is less empirical accuracy than the reality of events as they are encountered and delivered by a thinking, receiving subject and an active listener. As the artists in the exhibition ably demonstrate, storytelling need not be an escape into fantasy. Rather, it can serve as a way of both coming to terms with the world and giving it form—through personal narratives and unique encounters that intersect and unfold to create a multilayered experience of reality.

1 Walter Benjamin, "The Storyteller: Reflections on the Works of Nikolai Leskov," in *Selected Writings*, vol. 3, 1935-1938, ed. Michael W. Jennings, trans. Edmund Jephcott et al. (Cambridge, MA and London, England: The Belknap Press of Harvard University Press, 2002), 146.

2 As the French philosopher Jacques Rancière observed, "an emancipated community is in fact a community of storytellers and translators." Rancière, "The Emancipated Spectator," *Artforum* (March 2007): 280. For more on the relationship between Rancière's work and the use of storytelling in contemporary art, see T.J. Demos's "Storytelling in/as Contemporary Art" in this publication.

3 Benjamin, "The Storyteller," 143.

4 Paul Ricoeur, "Life in Quest of Narrative," in
David Wood ed., *On Paul Ricoeur: Narrative and
Interpretation* (London: Routledge, 1991), 20-33.

5 Benjamin, "The Storyteller," 146.

6 Claire Gilman and Margaret Sundell, Interview with
Missing Books (August 10, 2007).

7 Joachim Koester, Artist Statement accompanying the
exhibition of *The Kant Walks* at Galleri Nicolai Wallner,
Copenhagen, Denmark, 2005, n.p.

8 Michel de Certeau, "Spatial Stories," in *The Practice of
Everyday Life* (Berkeley and Los Angeles: University of
California Press, 1988), 115-130.

9 Koester, Artist Statement.

10 Margaret Sundell, "1000 Words: Liisa Roberts talks
about *What's the Time in Vyborg?*," *Artforum* (March
2004): 153.

11 Benjamin, "The Storyteller," 149.

12 J.R.R. Tolkien, "On Fairy Stories," in *The Tolkien Reader*
(New York: Ballantine Books, 1966), 54ff.

13 Steve Mumford, *Baghdad Journal: An Artist in Occupied
Iraq* (Montreal: Drawn & Quarterly Books, 2005), 21.

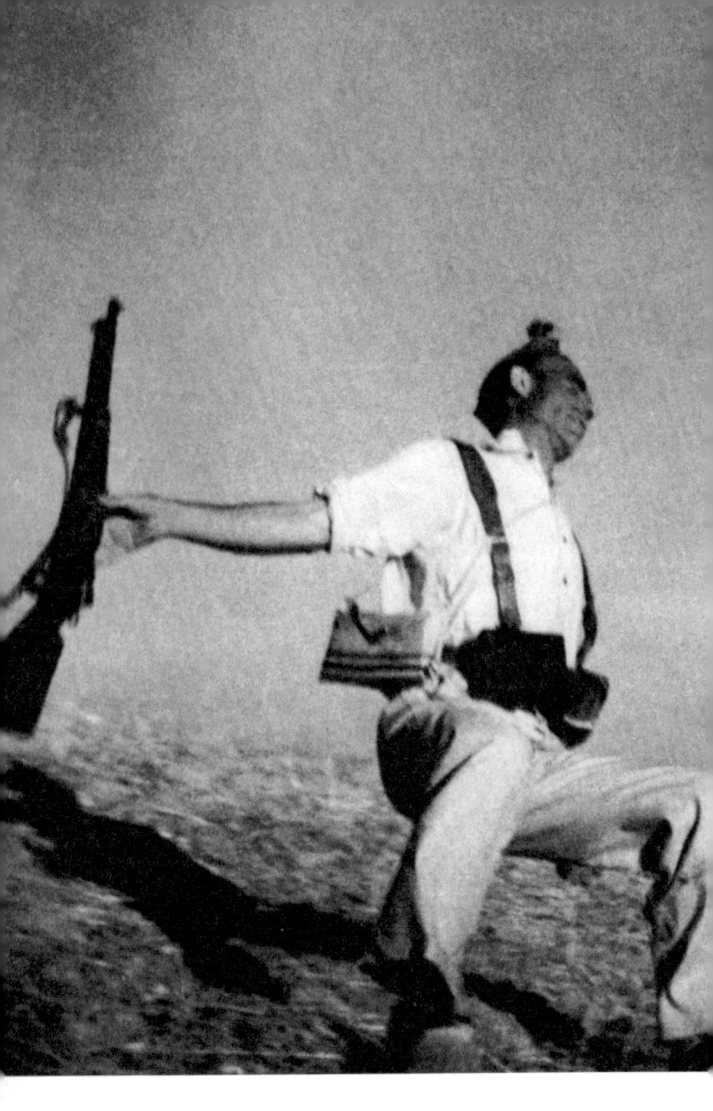

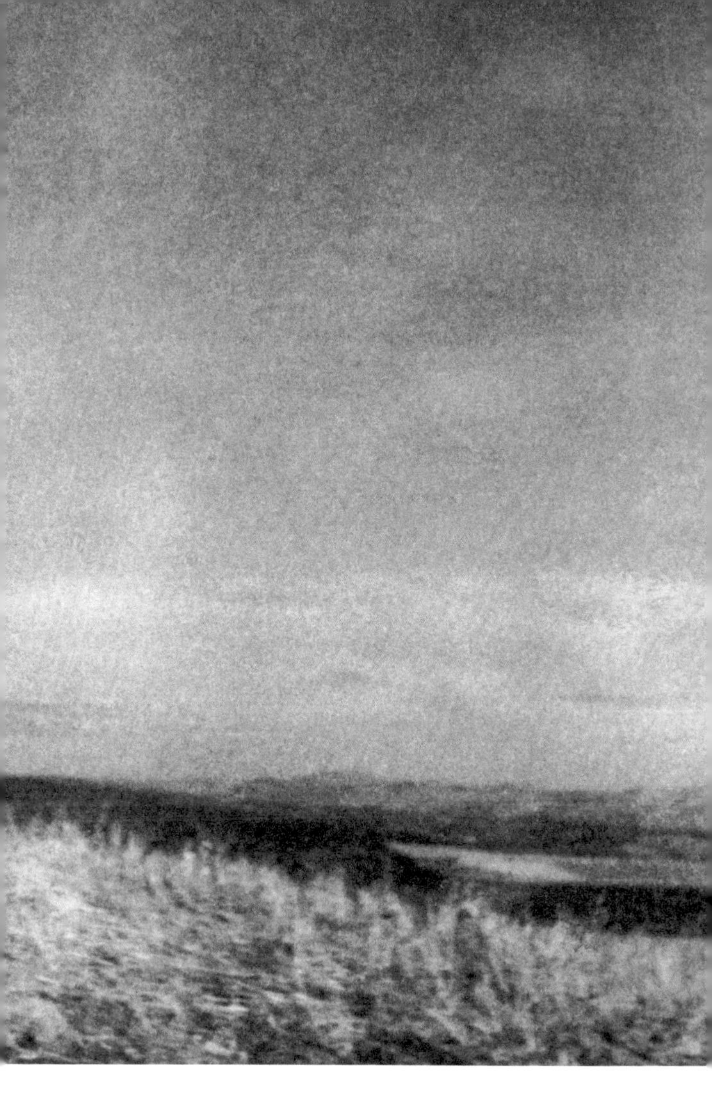

← ROBERT CAPA, *Death of a Loyalist Militiaman
(Falling Soldier)*, 1936

72

What is it?: The Image, Between Documentary and Near Documentary

Okwui Enwezor

A great specter currently haunts contemporary art: the specter of documentary forms, which range from documentary photography to narrative structures that deploy the recursive registers of historical recollection. Of course, such forms, whether pictorial or narrative, are not new to the production of art, as the genealogy of history painting and the ethnography of 17th-century genre scenes make obvious. What makes recent forms of documentary of interest is the degree to which they respond to a visual field inundated by images of different orders of truth, veracity, authenticity, and reality. (Think, for example, of the flourishing of reality television.) The modern documentary is caught between the poles of the testamentary and the evidentiary, between an over-identification with eye-witness accounts and the detached objective view of photojournalism. This entanglement places the documentary in conflict with the supposed autonomy of the work of art, especially with regards to art's assumed distance from the real and journalistic in favor of the imaginative and speculative.

Recent attempts to place the documentary within the production and practices of art seem to ask: to what degree does the documentary respond to this dichotomy? For more than a century, contemporary art, particularly photography, has been awash in a sea of documentary strategies: consider the soft-focus pictorialism of Alfred Stieglitz; the photomontages of the 1920s and 1930s in Germany and Russia; Pop art, Conceptualism, the post-Conceptual appropriationist practices of the Pictures generation of the 1970s; the pictorial, large-format, absorptive imagery of the 1990s; the scrappy, politically inflected investigations of non-objective documentary formats. Such photography includes, in one form or other, (but surely is not limited to) the documentary.

Among the forms of documentary practices, namely those methods that pay close attention to realism or visual manifestations that corroborate an objective image and its representation, the one that is most intriguing for our purposes is what the artist Jeff Wall named "near documentary." Here, Wall described an image regime that closely follows the conventions of documentary photography but is deeply ambivalent about the veracity of what it describes. The fundamental principle of such an image and the motivation for its production is that its scenario be plausible, namely that what it captures describes something and reflects a kind of truth that is already transparent to the general culture, even though it may never have existed in reality. There are other forms of near documentary following Wall's terms, especially of the anthropological and ethnographic kind, such as Cindy Sherman's nonrealistic post-portraits or James Casebere's and Thomas Demand's photographs, which construct a view of the real as models that are photographed. Each of these practices deals with the artifice of artistic production. They wager nothing in terms of claims of veracity, authenticity, truth, or the real since their conventions spring from the history of art, even if they borrow from the toolkit of the documentarist. To that extent it is difficult to think of contemporary art today, as Michael Fried recently argued, without confronting the enervating intrusion of photography and the role it plays in image making.

While the sea change in contemporary art heralded by photography has been around since the days of Walter Benjamin, it is only recently that photography's muscular ascendancy as a major medium of artistic practice has become clearer and canonically relevant. With this shift from a minor medium—which positioned photography as secondary to the modernist concerns of originality—the discursive conditions of the photographic form have become more complex. As artists veer away from the formalist edifices and traditional pictorialism of large-format photography and immersive cinemascope video projections toward more narrative-driven documentary approaches, a schism in the theorization and analysis of the discursive conditions of photographic practice forces a reconsideration of its formats. Over the last decade, an increasing shift toward the documentary has provoked debate about the very status of the photographic image's claim as art. It is a fruitful area that *The Storyteller* boldly enters, the more to investigate a rising apperception of the properties of the documentary within the categories of contemporary artistic practice.

Two issues that seem to make the art world uncomfortable with the documentary, despite, as *The Storyteller* shows, the proliferation of interest in its methods in recent work, are its relationship to politics and its connection to commodity. These issues have been further exacerbated by the anxious tendency of formalist criticism to depoliticize the documentary in favor of the pictorial. By the same token, it is the tendency of documentary practices to animate and privilege considerations of the political, whether visually or discursively, over conventional visual regimes of art. Art, it is often said, must stand apart and outside the real in order to penetrate reality with its subversive interruption of society's received truths. On the other hand, in a world in which the image is a dominant part of everyday social interaction, artists see no reason why documentary and art should be in conflict.

However, this shift toward deploying documentary strategies—even when employed in works that are not, strictly speaking, documentary— has occurred at a time in which, especially beyond the artistic sphere, the documentary has been in crisis. So many questions about classic images of documentary photography have been raised over the years, sometimes challenging the very foundation on which the documentary rests—namely its corroborative capacity to place the photographer at the center of historical events and viewers in proximity to the distilled experience captured by the photographer. These questions are not pedestrian. They are both philosophical and epistemological. They hint at the believability of the stated scenarios of iconic images.

One such question concerns hedging—or, as the case may be, fudging. Consider the case of Robert Capa's *Falling Soldier*, a monument of 20th-century war photography. One of the questions this photograph has raised since it was first published 73 years ago—and, more insistently, since the 1970s—concerns its authenticity. Is the photograph real or fake? Or, to apply Wall's term: is it a documentary or near documentary? In near documentary parlance, there is no controversy, since wars happen, soldiers get shot, and some kind of story always needs to be told about the misery of war. But in documentary terms, the issue is far more serious, too reductive to parse: Did this happen? Did the photographer see it happen? Is the image a direct, unadulterated record of the event as it occurred? In other words, the questions are not about the seeming plausibility of an image but the veracity of the pictorial account.

In a recent report in *The New York Times* (August 17, 2009), questions were raised anew about the authenticity of *Falling Soldier*. The photograph depicts, against a stark, eerily lit, picturesque backdrop, the balletic grace of a man struck by a powerful bullet. The man, wearing a white shirt with rolled sleeves and a pair of loose-fitting khaki fatigue pants, is pitched backward by the force of the bullet, his arms flung out, his right hand clutching a rifle that will soon be separated from his grip. This image of a man caught in the split second between life and death carries with it the authority of the documentary tradition that came to prominence in the midst of the brutality and devastation of the wars of the 20th century.

Falling Soldier, the photograph that propelled the young Capa, then only 22 years old, to international acclaim, is the kind of image of opportunity that is every photographer's dream. Such images are part of the glamour and mythology of documentary and war photography, and photojournalists are often the heroes who risk everything, including their lives, to reveal such intimate moments. Capa is an iconic figure of the documentary tradition. His war photography—from the Spanish Civil War to the landing on Normandy Beach during World War II to the First Indochina War (where Capa met his own early death in Vietnam in 1954)—is considered seminal; his place in the history of 20th-century documentary photography is further cemented by the fact that he was one of the founders of Magnum, the premier agency of documentary photographers.

The *Times* article recounts the claim by a Spanish researcher, José Manuel Susperregui, that Capa's famous image, photographed on September 5, 1936 (only two months after the Spanish Civil War began), was staged. This claim was not the first time doubt was raised about the authenticity of the image—or, rather, the authenticity of the documented event represented in the image. What made Susperregui's claim intriguing to experts willing to reconsider what may have seemed a settled precedent was his research into the circumstances and location of the picture. Susperregui, like a forensic crime scene investigator, had superimposed images of the landscape at Cerro Muriano (near Córdoba), where *Falling Soldier* supposedly was shot, and found profound dissimilarities between the photograph's more rugged landscape and the actual wooded landscape of Cerro Muriano, which, Capa's caption claims, was where the photograph was taken. According to Susperregui's research, the image was not photographed at Cerro Muriano but at Espejo, a town 35 miles away. If this is indeed the case, and if the image was made at the time Capa claimed it was, then it was surely a staged enactment since no fighting had taken place at Espejo at the time the photograph was made. Still, is it possible that Capa took the picture at Espejo, but in the rush of dispatching the image to press erroneously misattributed the event as having occurred at Cerro Muriano? It's also possible that Capa—or someone else—made a mistake about the date.

Whatever conclusions are reached about the authenticity/veracity/truthfulness/realness of the photograph, the more immediate question *Falling Soldier* raises is whether an image can be false in its details but true in the substance of its pictorial address. In this case we are confronted with the full dimension of what is often designated as documentary, in the terms put forward by the inflections and hermeneutic functions of the terms authenticity/veracity/truthfulness/realness of an image. Capa's *Falling Soldier* is seen by historians of documentary photography as a historical monument, a foundational and archetypal image of the genre of photojournalism. In this regard, Capa's photograph is more than a symbol of the role of the photographer as a witness of events of historic magnitude; it is a sacred object of the ethical clarity of the documentary purpose.

The issues are of course complex. Whatever the outcome of the analysis, there is still no incontrovertible evidence that *Falling Soldier* was staged. Even if it was, it strikes me that Capa was aiming less at documentary verisimilitude and more at near-documentary plausibility. In this sense, *The Storyteller* seeks to direct our attention to the ways in which the terms of documentary are easily subverted by deviation from its classic forms by having us consider the way images are embedded into narrative channels that vitiate all authoritative considerations of the authenticity/veracity/truthfulness/realness of the documentary object.

Storytelling in/as Contemporary Art

T.J. Demos

An emancipated community is in fact a
community of storytellers …
—Jacques Rancière[1]

Since the mid-1990s, and particularly in the last few years, storytelling has been gaining growing momentum in contemporary art. Indeed, it has proliferated internationally in numerous mediums—the video-essay, the photographic cycle, the pictorial series in drawing and painting, as well as in performance and theater, to name a few. But whereas storytelling might at first call up fairytales and the communal transmission of collective memory—in other words, traditional rituals that are distinctly anti-modern—contemporary art confers on its practice an experimental, innovative cast, producing socially relevant and politically engaged work. As the work assembled in *The Storyteller* by Claire Gilman and Margaret Sundell demonstrates, artists today are likely to tell stories that confront geopolitical events, related, for instance, to the trauma of military and social

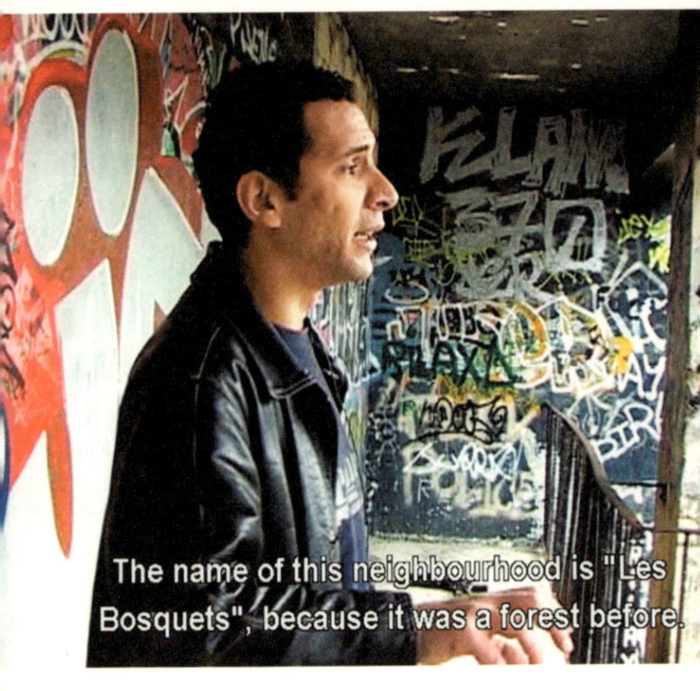

EMANUEL LICHA, *War Tourist in the Suburbs of Paris*, 2004–2008 (video still)

HITO STEYERL, *Journal No. 1 — An Artist's Impression*, 2007 (video still) → → →

84

conflict or to complex political transitions. The models of storytelling they employ are typically couched in subjective presentations, are experiential and memory-based, and involve various modalities of the sayable and visible that tend to reject history's official, definitive, and objective character. As such, storytelling in contemporary art generally mingles literary, essayistic, and performative registers, and is frequently developed via moving images (e.g., film and video) or series of representations (in photography, painting, and drawing), which are able to extend a plot across time, building multiple strands of meaning over an array of images.

As such, storytelling has reflected and responded to transformations in global society over the last 20 years, a period marked by the fall of the Berlin Wall, the dissolution of the Soviet Union, and the cultural and economic liberalization of China. In addition to the rise of political Islam, the destruction of the World Trade Center, and the subsequent wars in Iraq and Afghanistan, the last two decades have defined a conflicted period of globalization, from Clinton's neoliberal capitalism to Bush's neoconservative imperialism. It has involved worldwide economic inequality, failed states in Africa and autocratic regimes in the Middle East, and the mounting catastrophe of global warming. Despite massive uprisings against Bush's invasions and mobilizations for global justice and ecological sustainability world-wide, there has been a growing detachment between social movements and the course of government actions.

This widespread failure of political inclusivity has no doubt fueled the turn to storytelling. Faced with the alienation from the official narratives of government—which have proved, at times, disastrously misguided yet nonetheless powerful in drowning out opposition—and confronted by the stultifying exposure to the consumerist spectacle of mainstream corporate news, many people encounter a resulting cynicism when they find that their experiences are consistently disregarded by political representatives and mass media. Such disillusionment has led to profound disaffection, but it has also stoked the desire for the emancipation from official histories. This desire has lead to alternative forms of knowledge production, to new histories that include those who have suffered or otherwise been rendered invisible, as well as to innovative ways of relaying experience by rethinking representation.

In this regard, the artistic practice of storytelling builds on related artistic trends in recent years.

For instance, identifying an "archival impulse" in contemporary art, Hal Foster has highlighted how artists make constructive connections between disparate images and objects—whether in the film, installation art, or sculpture of such figures as Tacita Dean, Sam Durant, and Thomas Hirschhorn—by which lost artifacts and disjunctive signs are recovered and realigned, and are thereby "retrieved in a gesture of alternative knowledge or counter-memory."[2] Artists like Dean, moreover, frequently acknowledge their debt to such writers as J.G. Ballard and W.G. Sebald, who similarly emphasize subjective recollection and gripping narratives in their semi-fictional prose. Defying the schizophrenic conditions of spatial fragmentation and historical amnesia that reigned during the postmodernism of the 1980s, the archival impulse is joined by methods of "postproduction"—the reuse of existing imagery, as in digital sampling and MP3 mixing beginning in the early 1990s—in order to construct new scenarios and creative social relations for comprehending and experiencing the world, as curator Nicolas Bourriaud argues.[3] Lastly, artists have also pursued resolutely historical projects in a variety of mediums, according to which "historical research and representation appear central," as art historian Mark Godfrey notes in relation to the films of Matthew Buckingham.[4]

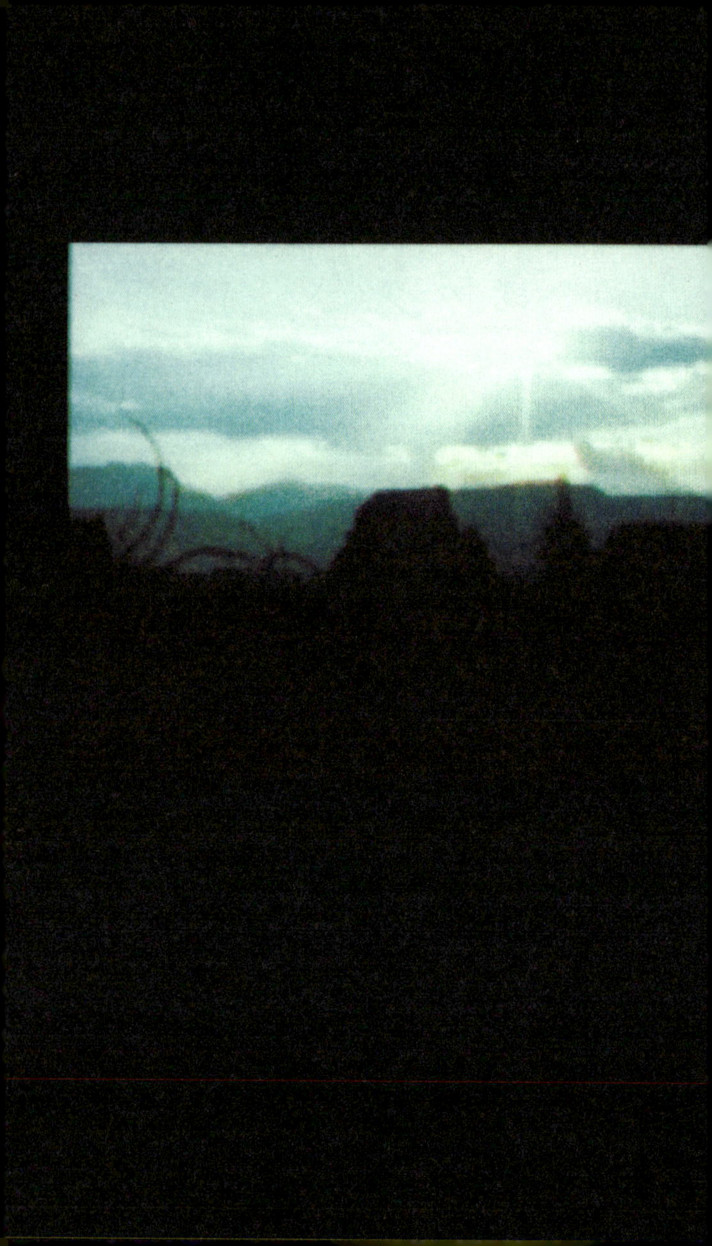

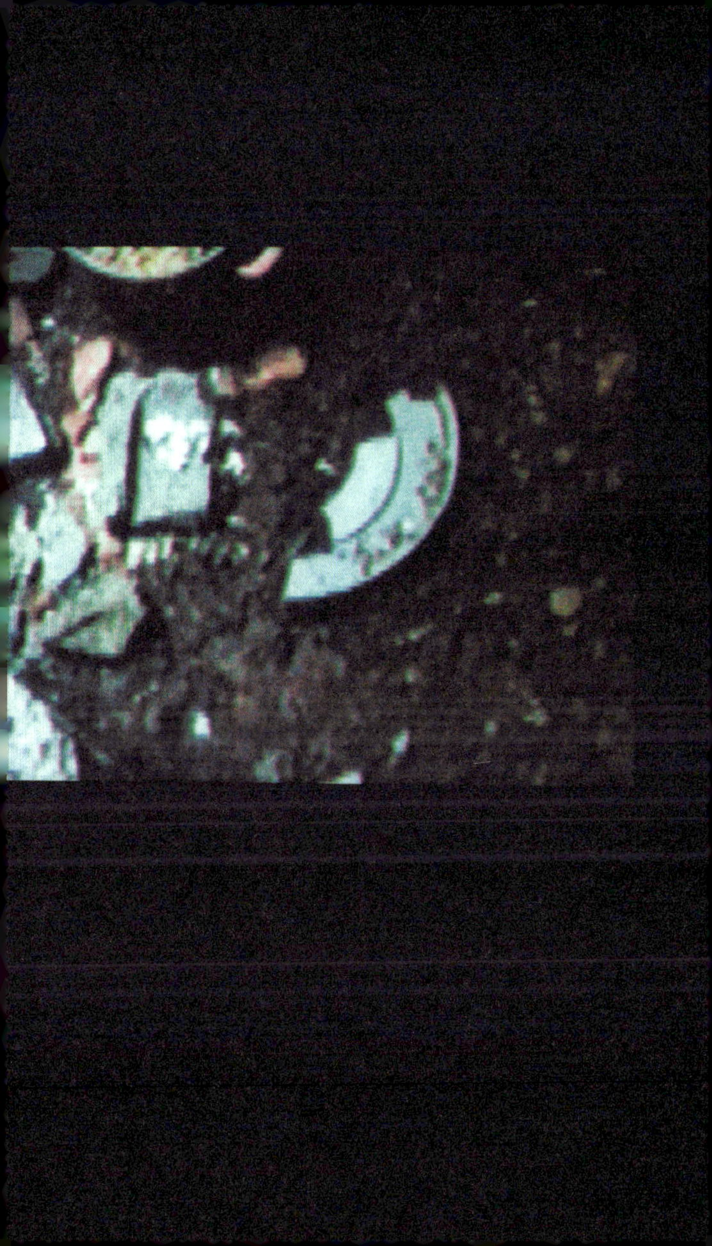

In these interrelated trends—the archival impulse, postproduction, and the artist as historian—the prevalent attention to drawing connections across heterogeneous objects, images, and contexts is also shared by storytelling, which partakes of all these models. Consider among *The Storyteller*'s featured works Lamia Joreige's archive of civil war recollections, Hito Steyerl's digital re-montage of historical imagery in her videos, or Emanuel Licha's historiographic revisitation of post-conflict sites in Paris following the uprising of the city's North African community in response to police oppression and discrimination in France. What all share are the markers of storytelling—the building of a riveting plotline, the visualization of past events, the immersive experience of narrative duration.

Indeed, experiencing the moving accounts of others—whether concerning Joreige's Lebanon, Steyerl's Balkans, or Licha's Paris—elicits a certain transformative power, one of mobile identifications, imaginative fantasy, and collective bonding. Perhaps this power is not so distant from that which characterized the tradition of storytelling that Walter Benjamin famously argued was irrevocably damaged in the modern conditions of traumatic violence, as during World War I.[5] No doubt today's context is very different, particularly since current storytelling is not so much debilitated by conflict as instrumentalized in mainstream cinema and television, which offer sources of virtual entertainment removed from reality's social discord, and thereby allow conflict to continue outside its walls. In this regard, it is important to signal the frequent oppositional relation of artistic storytelling today to the narratives of the culture industry and its largely consensual community of escapist enjoyment and fantasy—particularly when Hollywood commonly ignores or rewrites historical fact, endowing its films with hackneyed characters and happy endings. Yet, while contemporary artists adopt methods of reflexive criticality to challenge the spectator's potential thoughtless immersion within mainstream consumerist spectacle, they tend also to reject an earlier anti-aesthetic opposition to narrative in favor of creative forms of fabulation that make their regard for the narrative power of Hollywood films more complex. The relation between experimental art and the culture industry is therefore different from that in previous decades: whereas once avant-garde filmmakers (for example, Peter Gidal, Hollis Frampton, and Laura Mulvey) criticized narrative cinema for participating in a logic that correlated visual

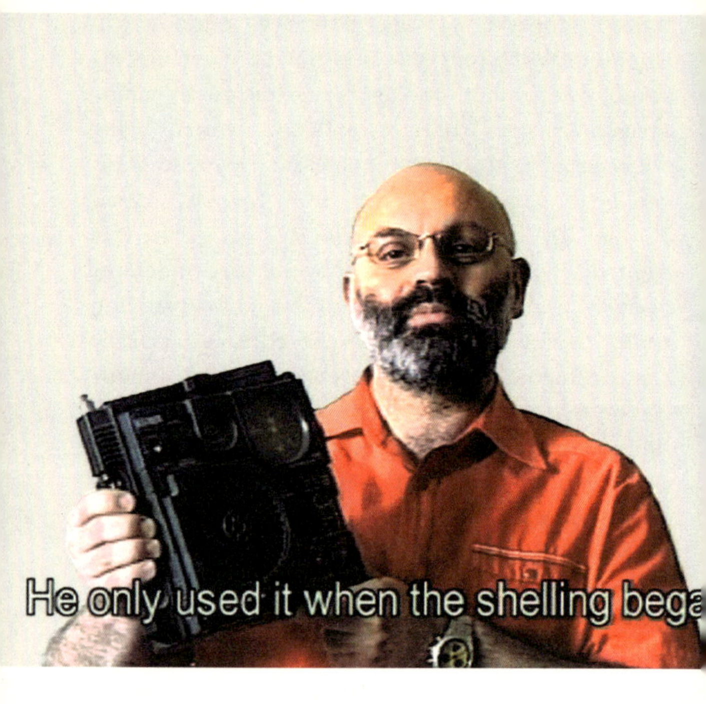

LAMIA JOREIGE, *Objects of War n° 3*, 2006 (video still)

pleasure and society's oppressive social conventions of inequality (in terms of film's facilitating
the viewer's identification with racist and sexist
identities),[6] current practitioners—as is evident
here—resist overestimating anti-narrative techniques that would refuse any and all storytelling
as merely conservative.

How might we characterize the specific nature of
current modes of narration? Writing during the
1980s about film, the philosopher Gilles Deleuze
compared the "organic narration" of what he
termed the "movement-image" of classic cinema
(e.g., the films of Alfred Hitchcock) to the "crystalline narration" of the "time-image" of post-
WWII cinema (e.g., the French new wave films of
Alain Resnais and Jean-Luc Godard)—the first
designating a mode of storytelling by which
characters react clearly to situations with a
beginning, middle, and end; the second, an unfolding of pure optical and sound events to which
the characters do not necessarily respond, and
where image, event, and character become
"delinked."[7] Whereas Deleuze understood this
historical shift to be cinema's progressive development, philosopher Jacques Rancière has
argued more recently that these forms represent two simultaneously present aspects of
film—which in fact corresponds precisely to the

complex narrative directions of contemporary art. By mixing organic and crystalline narration, artists today tend to fabricate illusive plotlines even while they experiment with temporal duration, desynchronize relations between sounds and visions, and blur the distinctions between the imaginative and the documentary. Exemplary is Adrian Paci's *Albanian Stories*, which presents a video recording of his daughter telling a seemingly folkloric tale. Situated in the space and experimental context of contemporary art by virtue of her father's video, however, the piece takes on an allusive and self-reflexive character, as it joins the girl's references to the geopolitical turbulence of her native Eastern Europe with the artistic critique of representation, evident in the video's stress on her fragmented rendition, which is filled with gaps and ambiguities.

Consequently, the art of storytelling reveals, more often than not, a rupture in its representation (such as fragmentation, interruptive montage, inexplicable intervals) that emphasizes the non-closure of tales. Similarly, storytelling courts a heterogeneity of sources (including drawings of photographs and mixtures of documentary footage and fictional frameworks) that, in refusing seamless joints, questions the

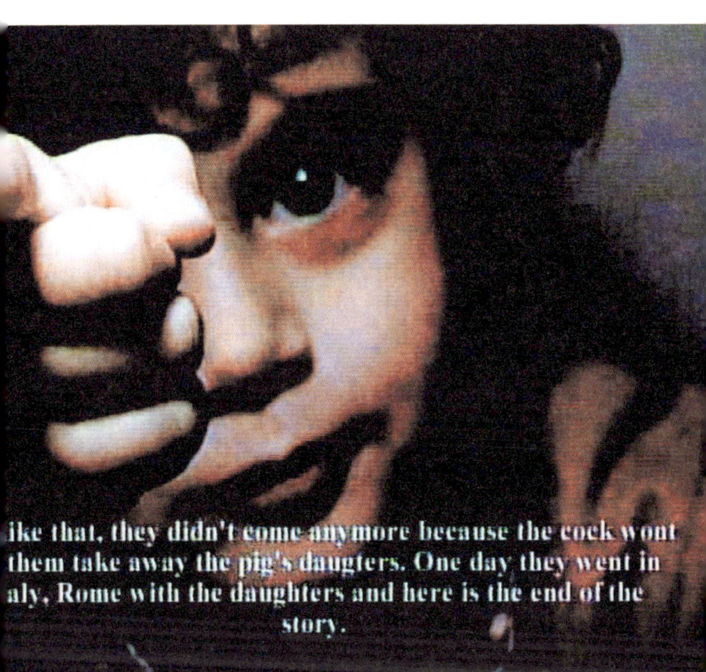

ADRIAN PACI, *Albanian Stories*, 1997 (video still)

security and epistemological stability of any one of them. In doing so, the art of storytelling enacts a paradoxical coupling of narrative and opacity, of making connections between diverse images and questioning definitive conclusions. This double tendency goes to the very heart of the cinematic for Rancière, who argues that film is an essential form of storytelling today insofar as it unites what he terms the "representational regime," relating to narrative, meaning, and identification, with the "aesthetic regime," designating the realm of sensation, affect, and opacity.[8] The combination brings about two outcomes that are valid for contemporary storytelling in general.

First, the simultaneity of narrative engagement and representational breakdown leads frequently to an allegorical mode of storytelling, one concerned with the story's discrepancies and a questioning of the image's truthfulness in relation to the chronology of events or the psychology of participants, as mentioned above.[9] For instance, Omer Fast's *Spielberg's List* elicits the ambiguity between Holocaust survivors' memories of the Auschwitz concentration camp and recollections of their involvement as extras in the making of the Hollywood film *Schindler's List*, an ambiguity that manifests itself in the

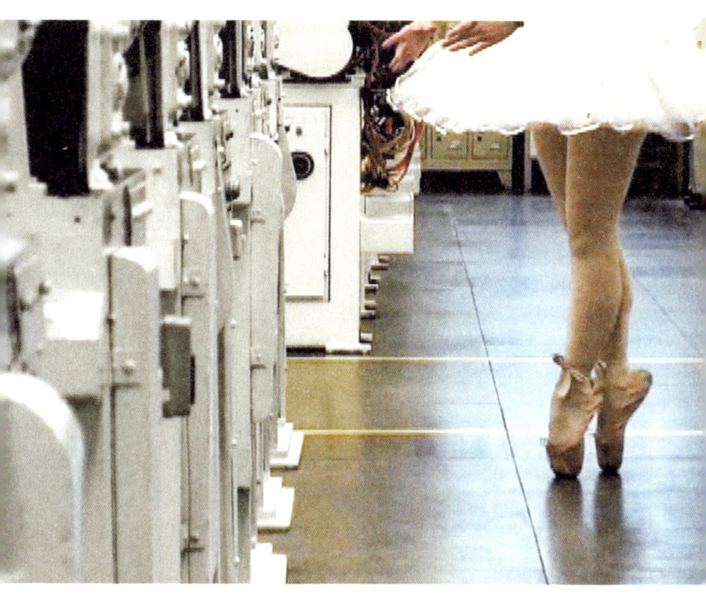

CAO FEI, *Whose Utopia*, 2006 (video still)

JEREMY DELLER AND MIKE FIGGIS, *The Battle of Orgreave*, 2002 (details of production stills) → → →

confusion of words and contexts (e.g., whether one was "shot" by a guard during WWII or by Spielberg's camera). Exemplifying the tendency of storytelling to present a self-critical narration, reflexive in its use of forms and conventions, Fast's double video projection results in many stories about stories.[10] Second, whereas storytelling might suggest a world of make-believe, the use of fiction in contemporary art actually remains connected to the world of socio-political reality, suggesting a mode of construction, of building new ways of comprehending events and organizing memories. Indeed, for Rancière, "fiction" is not a matter of semblance and artifice; rather, its origin lies in the Latin *fingere*, meaning "to forge," not "to feign": "fiction means using the means of art to construct a 'system' of represented actions, assembled forms, and internally coherent signs," he explains.[11]

As a result, the art of storytelling proposes a modeling of truth that differs from previous post-Enlightenment paradigms (such as Freudian, criminological, and art-historical models).[12] Instead of defining truth as representative of an already existing reality, to which the image corresponds as a faithful copy, current modes of storytelling inaugurate a new reality and a new community, according to which truth emerges as in-process, contingent, and intrinsic to social and political struggle.[13] Liberated from its basis in re-presenting past events, fiction's constructivist power means that its stories can authorize imaginative futures—as when Cao Fei transforms China's oppressive industrial reality of dehumanizing production into the stage for imaginative realizations in her video *Whose Utopia*. As philosopher Michel Foucault wrote in relation to what he saw as a new "politics of truth," it is not a matter of simply determining "the conditions and the limits of our possible knowledge of the object"—as in past epistemological models (for instance, of modernist critique); rather, we must "seek the conditions and the indefinite possibilities of transforming the subject, of transforming ourselves."[14]

If the truth of storytelling unleashes a power that transforms the subject and transforms ourselves, it can be said to found a community in the act of sharing experience. This does not mean, however, that storytelling establishes mere consensus, for many the basis of post-politics today, according to which the pressure of social unity drives out disagreement and introduces a depoliticized ethical accord, one that creates the conditions for "pre-emptive

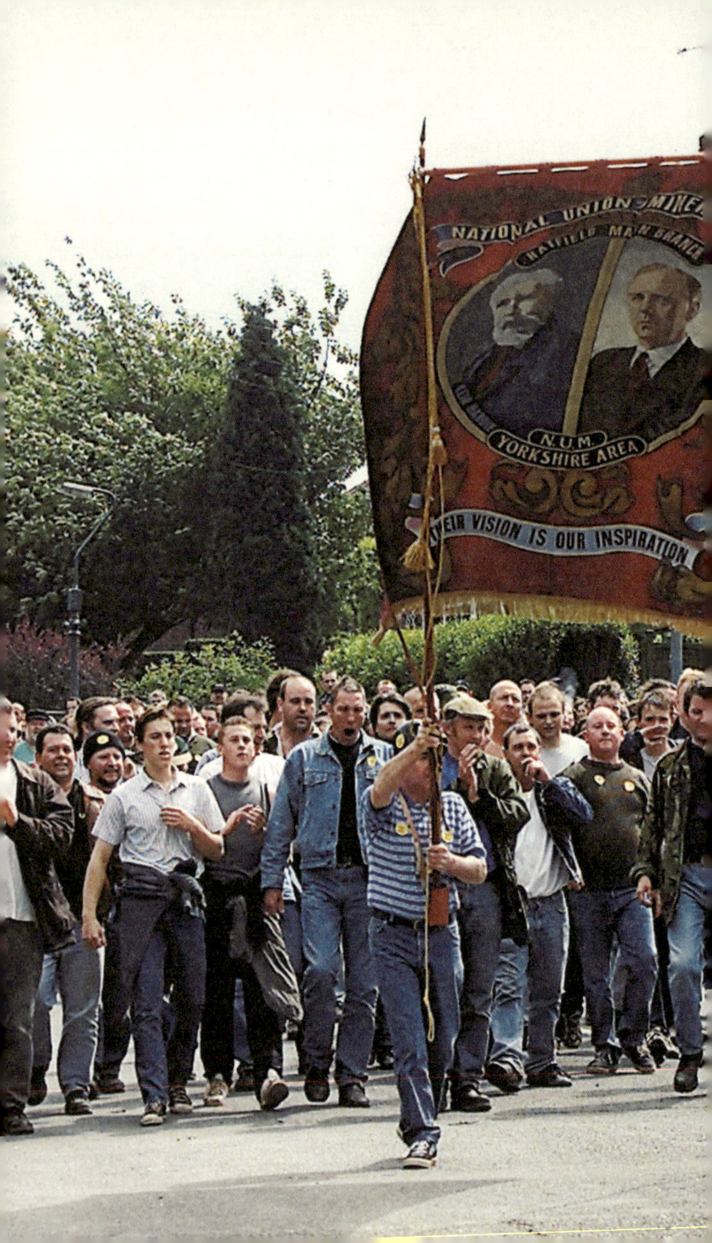

NATIONAL UNION MINE
HATFIELD MAIN BRANCH
N.U.M.
YORKSHIRE AREA
THEIR VISION IS OUR INSPIRATION

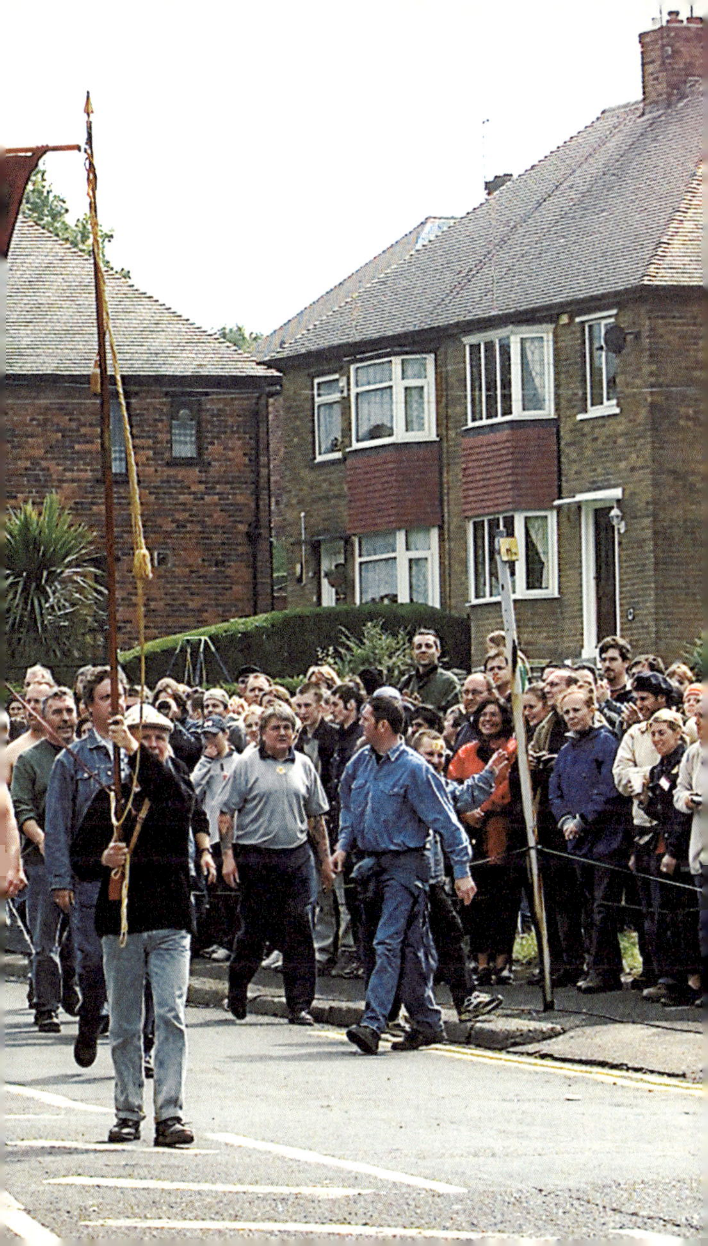

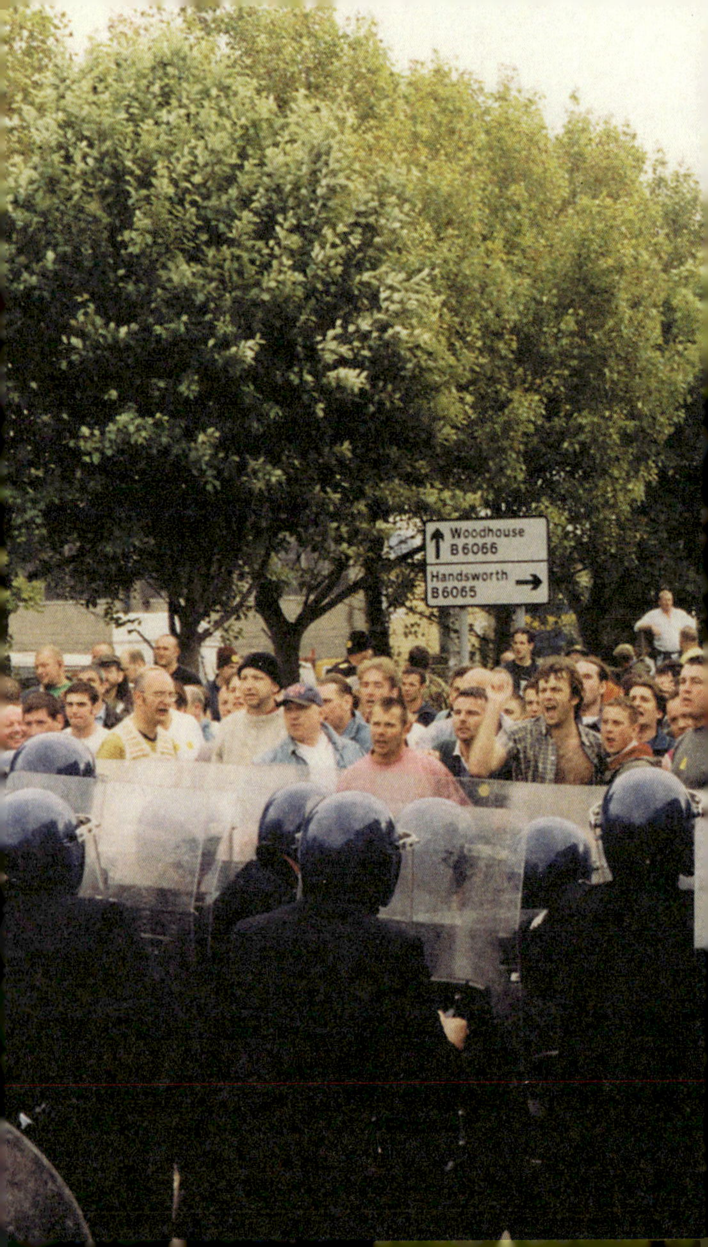
Woodhouse
B 6066
Handsworth
B 6065

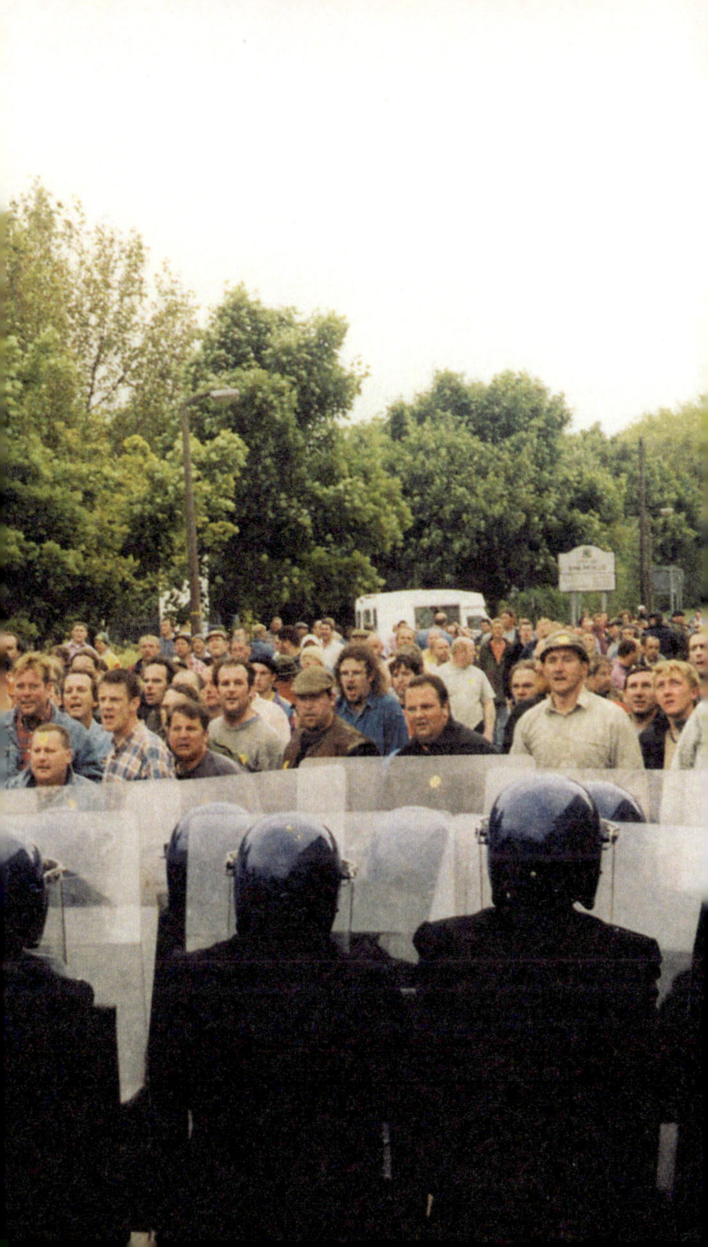

actions, legitimized assassinations, calculatedly uneven distribution of goods, humanitarian war against those suppressing the rights of man, and so forth"[15]—in other words, the precarious state of government after September 11, 2001. Rather, experimental storytelling can found communities organized around the disappeared (as when the collective Missing Books republishes a text by Rodolfo Walsh, who was shot by agents of the Argentine military dictatorship in 1977), communities of oppositional social movements (as when Jeremy Deller re-enacted a British miners' protest), communities critical of ethnic segregation (as when Hito Steyerl interrogates the post-war ethnic divisions of former Yugoslavian populations), or communities of the politically excluded (as when Michael Rakowitz imports Iraqi dates to the US for the first time in a quarter of a century).

Yet perhaps the most important key to disrupting the simple consensus of traditional modes of narration is to reject the conventional division between the artist-as-storyteller and the viewer-as-audience. As Rancière contends, emancipation comes only when we all become storytellers—that is, when the audience joins the artist in the act of producing meaning. Indeed, storytelling creates a context for imaginative invention as much as a suggestive recounting of past events. If the art of telling stories is pre-eminently about creating "shared forms of life,"[16] even if provisional, as Rancière argues, it is because it enables "spectators who are active interpreters, who render their own translation, who appropriate the story for themselves, and who ultimately make their own story out of it."[17] This openness lends itself in the best of cases to a culture of collective engagement, aesthetic creativity, and political becoming, where storytelling is practiced by all.

1 Jacques Rancière, "The Emancipated Spectator," *Artforum* (March 2007): 280.

2 Hal Foster, "An Archival Impulse," *October* 110 (Fall 2004): 4.

3 See Fredric Jameson, "The Cultural Logic of Late Capitalism," in *Postmodernism, or The Cultural Logic of Late Capitalism* (Durham: Duke University Press, 1992); and Nicolas Bourriaud, *Postproduction: Culture as Screenplay: How Art Reprograms the World*, trans. Caroline Schneider (New York: Lukas & Sternberg, 2002).

4 Mark Godfrey, "The Artist as Historian," *October* 120 (Spring 2007): 142-143.

5 See Walter Benjamin, "The Storyteller: Reflections on the Works of Nikolai Leskov," in *Illuminations*, trans. Harry Zohn (New York: Schocken Books, 1968).

6 See Laura Mulvey, "Visual Pleasure and Narrative Cinema," *Screen*, 16/3 (Autumn 1975): 6-18.

7 See Gilles Deleuze, *Cinema 2: The Time-Image*, trans. Hugh Tomlinson and Robert Galeta (Minneapolis: University of Minnesota Press, 1989). See esp. 128ff.

8 For Brian Massumi, affect designates intensity via sensation, outside of emotional, psychological coding. See his essay "The Autonomy of Affect," in *Parables for the Virtual: Movement, Affect, Sensation* (Durham: Duke University Press, 2002).

9 As in Buckingham's work, which represents, according to Godfrey, "stories about the past, and often previously unacknowledged ones—all the while subjecting conventional modes of narrative and historiography to critical scrutiny." (Godfrey, "The Artist as Historian," 170). On allegory, see Craig Owens, "The Allegorical Impulse: Toward a Theory of Postmodernism," *October* 12 (Spring 1980): 67-86.

10 In this regard, we might identify a historical development from "pictures" to "stories"—that is, from what Douglas Crimp considered the shift in the late 1970s toward the singular image of the "picture" (behind which, for Crimp, there is always another image) to today's focus on "stories" (which always connect to other stories). See Douglas Crimp, "Pictures," *October* 8 (Spring 1979): 75-88.

11 Jacques Rancière, "Documentary Fiction: Marker and the Fiction of Memory," in *Film Fables*, trans. Emiliano Battista (Oxford, UK: Berg Publishers, 2006), 158. Like the storyteller, Godfrey's artist-as-historian also turns "to fiction not in order to evade historical representation but to represent historical experience more adequately." (Godfrey, "The Artist as Historian," 145).

12 On these models of truth, see Carlo Ginzburg, "Clues: Morelli, Freud, and Sherlock Holmes," in *The Sign of Three: Dupin, Holmes, Peirce*, ed. Umberto Eco and Thomas A. Sebeok (Bloomington: Indiana University Press, 1988).

13 Cf. Deleuze, *Cinema 2*: "Thus the cinema can call itself *cinéma-vérité*, all the more because it will have destroyed every model of the true so as to become creator and producer of truth: this will not be a cinema of truth but the truth of cinema" (151).

14 Michel Foucault, "Subjectivity and Truth," in *The Politics of Truth*, ed. Sylvère Lotringer, trans. Lysa Hochroth and Catherine Porter (Los Angeles: Semiotext(e), 2007), 152-53.

15 Tom Conley, "Cinema and its Discontents: Jacques Rancière and Film Theory," *SubStance* 108 (2005): 103.

16 Rancière, *Film Fables*, 177.

17 Ibid., 280.

List of Works Exhibited and Reproduced

Note: height precedes width precedes depth; all dimensions provided are for unframed work unless otherwise specified.

CAO FEI
Born 1978, Guangzhou, China
Lives in Beijing

Whose Utopia, 2006
Single-channel video with color and sound
20 minutes
Courtesy of the artist and Lombard-Freid Projects,
New York

JEREMY DELLER AND MIKE FIGGIS
Born 1966, London, and 1948, Carlisle, United Kingdom
Both live in London

The Battle of Orgreave, 2002
Single-channel video with color and sound
62 minutes
Courtesy of Artangel, London, and Channel 4

OMER FAST
Born 1972, Jerusalem
Lives in Berlin

Spielberg's List, 2005
Two-channel digital video with color and sound
65 minutes. Courtesy of Cine Plus, Berlin

MOUNIR FATMI
Born 1970, Tangier, Morocco
Lives in Paris

Save Manhattan 02, 2009
VHS tapes, glue, table
Approximately 60 x 91 x 37 in. (152 x 231 x 94 cm)
Courtesy of the artist and Lombard-Freid Projects, New York

RYAN GANDER
Born 1976, Chester, United Kingdom
Lives in Amsterdam and London

As Time Elapsed, 2005
31 books (*The Boy Who Always Looked Up*) on MDF shelf;
one viewing copy of *The Boy Who Always Looked Up*;
seven decks of playing cards
Approximately 18¹/₈ x 5¹/₈ x 7⁷/₈ in. (46 x 13 x 20 cm) overall
Courtesy of the artist; Tanya Bonakdar Gallery, New York;
Annet Gelink Gallery, Amsterdam; Lisson Gallery, London;
and Taro Nasu Gallery, Tokyo

LAMIA JOREIGE
Born 1972, Beirut, Lebanon
Lives in Beirut

Objects of War n° 3, 2006
Single-channel video with color and sound
55 minutes
Courtesy of the artist

Objects of War n° 4, 2006
Single-channel video with color and sound
72 minutes
Courtesy of the artist

JOACHIM KOESTER
Born 1962, Copenhagen, Denmark
Lives in New York

The Kant Walks, 2003
Seven chromogenic prints, two wall texts
Photographs: 18¹/₂ x 23¹/₂ in. each (47 x 59.7 cm)
Wall text: 11 x 8¹/₂ in. each (27.9 x 21.6 cm)

Courtesy of Greene Naftali, New York and the Martin Z.
Margulies Collection, Miami

EMANUEL LICHA
Born 1971, Montreal, Canada
Lives in Paris and Montreal

War Tourist in the Suburbs of Paris (one of five episodes
of the project *War Tourist*), 2004–2008
Single-channel video with color and sound
19 minutes, 42 seconds
Courtesy of the artist

MISSING BOOKS (MARIA BARNAS, MAXINE KOPSA,
GERMAINE KRUIP)
Formed and based in Amsterdam

Un Oscuro Día de Justicia (A Dark Day of Justice), 2005
Wood pallet, books by Rodolfo Walsh
Approximate overall dimensions: $31^{5}/_{8}$ × 42 × 36 in.
(80.3 × 106.7 × 91.4 cm)
Courtesy of the artists

In the Last 20 Minutes, 2005
Single-channel video with color and sound
21 minutes
Courtesy of the artists

STEVE MUMFORD
Born 1960, Boston
Lives in New York

2B4, Indoor Suq, Baghdad, August, 2003. (from the series
Iraq, 2003–2005), 2003
$13^{5}/_{8}$ × 11 in. (34.6 × 27.9 cm)

3B2, Bathers by the Tigris River, Baghdad. The soldiers, from the Florida National Guard's 3/124th infantry, were looking for weapons caches. (from the series *Iraq, 2003–2005*), 2003
11 x 13⁵/₈ in. (28 x 34.6 cm)

4B11, Men in Shabandar Teahouse, Sept, 2003. (from the series *Iraq, 2003–2005*), 2003
13⁵/₈ x 11 in. (13.6 x 27.9 cm)

4B7, Mosque on Firdos Sq, Baghdad, February, 2004. (from the series *Iraq, 2003–2005*), 2004
13⁵/₈ x 11 in. (34.6 x 27.9 cm)

4B15, Booksellers on Mutanebi Street laid their books out on the street every Friday morning. Many of my artist friends would meet each other here on these days. (from the series *Iraq, 2003–2005*), 2004
13³/₈ x 11 in. (34 x 28 cm)

9A6, Jean-Claude Chapon and Paul Garwood, reporters at FOB Iron Horse, Tikrit. March, 2004. (from the series *Iraq, 2003–2005*), 2004
11 x 13⁵/₈ in. (27.9 x 34.6 cm)

10A4, Iraqi contractors waiting to be paid on a Friday morning, FOB Thunder. (from the series *Iraq, 2003–2005*), 2004
11 x 13³/₈ in. (28 x 34 cm)

11A2, Iraqi police barricade on Abu Nawas Street, Next to the Tigris River. These barricades were part of the elaborate defenses around the Palestine and Sheraton hotels. June, 2004. (from the series *Iraq, 2003–2005*), 2004
12¹/₄ x 15³/₄ in. (31.1 x 40 cm)

11A4, A building across from Ahmed's studio, off Nasser Square and near the Bab al-Sharji marketplace. (from the series *Iraq*, 2003–2005), 2004
15³/₄ x 12¹/₄ in. (40 x 31.1 cm)

13A3, John, a contractor, giving a firearms class to Iraqi police in Khalis, July, 2004. The Iraqis had to be convinced to replace the rifle stocks on their AKs for better aiming, although it didn't look as cool. (from the series *Iraq*, 2003–2005), 2004
12¹/₄ x 15³/₄ in. (31.1 x 40 cm)

13B4, Georgian (Republic of Georgia) snipers on the Hibhib police station roof watching a bomb discovered on the street being rigged to be "blown in place" by an EOD squad. (from the series *Iraq*, 2003–2005), 2004
12¹/₄ x 15⁷/₈ in. (31.1 x 15.8 cm)

14B4, Lt. Col. Bulimore, commander of Task Force 1/6, meets with the sheiks of Buritz to discuss money for local projects. The sheiks were always interested in my drawings and often asked for them as gifts. (from the series *Iraq*, 2003–2005), 2004
10³/₄ x 15 in. (27.3 x 38.1 cm)

All works watercolor and ink on paper
Courtesy of Postmasters Gallery, New York

ADRIAN PACI
Born 1969, Shkoder, Albania
Lives in Milan, Italy

Albanian Stories, 1997
Single-channel video with color and sound, 7 minutes
Courtesy of Galleria Francesca Kaufmann, Milan

MICHAEL RAKOWITZ
Born 1973, Great Neck, New York
Lives in Chicago

Return, 2006 and ongoing
Multimedia installation
Dimensions variable
Courtesy of the artist and Lombard-Freid Projects,
New York

LIISA ROBERTS
Born 1969, Paris
Lives in Helsinki, St Petersburg, and New York

What's the Time in Vyborg?, 2000–2004
Single-channel video with color and sound
87 minutes
Courtesy of the artist

HITO STEYERL
Born 1966, Munich, Germany
Lives in Berlin

Journal No. 1—An Artist's Impression, 2007
Single-channel video with color, black-and-white, and sound
21 minutes
Courtesy of the artist

This book is published to accompany the traveling exhibition *The Storyteller*, organized and circulated by iCI (Independent Curators International), New York

Acknowledgments

The Storyteller grows from a core concept that is refreshingly accessible to all: that contemporary artists are using narrative techniques to communicate about transformative events of the past few decades. The offshoots from this thematic core reach into theoretical, social, and political territory, loaded with compelling imagery, documentation, narratives, and ideas. The international lineup of artists, originating from diverse locations and cultures, reflects expansive and innovative thinking from start to finish. In its format as a largely video-based presentation, we always knew it would travel well, perhaps even to the places the artists were born. It is my hope that *The Storyteller* will be seen across the world, and that it will question, inflame, prod, and inform diverse audiences, as great exhibitions so often do.

This traveling exhibition and publication have been made possible because of the dedication and commitment of many people. On behalf of iCI's executive director Kate Fowle, Board of Trustees, and staff, I would like to extend the utmost gratitude to the exhibition's dynamic, indefatigable curators, Claire Gilman and Margaret Sundell. The breadth and depth of their knowledge has enlightened and inspired us all throughout the many phases of the project's development, and their kindness, good humor, and grace under pressure have endured throughout. We give thanks as well to T.J. Demos, lecturer in modern and contemporary art at the University of London, for his excellent text; and to our esteemed colleague Okwui Enwezor, who has not only contributed an essay to this publication but whose groundbreaking presentation in 2002, *Documenta XI*, laid some of the foundations for *The Storyteller*.

All of us at iCI convey our deep thanks to the supporters of the exhibition. A generous grant from The Andy Warhol Foundation for the Visual Arts early in *The Storyteller's* development has been instrumental to the project. In addition, we are grateful for funding from The Horace W. Goldsmith Foundation and for support from iCI Benefactors Agnes Gund, Gerrit and Sydie Lansing, and Barbara and John Robinson, and iCI Partners Carol and Les Ballard, Jill Brienza and Nicholas L. Daraviras, Susan and Jeremy Coote, T.A. Fassburg, Jean Minskoff Grant and T Grant, Laure Lim and Tom Laurie, Michele Peck, Mara Sandler, Ann and Mel Schaffer, Madeline and Leslie Stern, and Barbara Toll. We also extend enormous appreciation to the generous individuals who wish to remain anonymous and who came to the rescue at a critical moment to ensure that this publication would proceed as first envisioned.

iCI also expresses gratitude to the individual lenders and their staffs, who have allowed these works to travel for the two-year exhibition tour. We wish to acknowledge those who went above and beyond the call of duty: Jane Lombard and Lea Freid of Lombard-Freid Projects and, especially, their gallery director, Cristian Alexa; as well as Carol Greene and Jay Sanders of Greene Naftali Gallery. Our appreciation goes out to all the lenders to *The Storyteller*, to co-director James Lingwood, Tom Dingle, and Liz Johnson of Artangel; Cao Fei; Ralph Neibuhr of Cine Plus Media Project; Mounir Fatmi and his studio assistant Aline Biasutto; Ryan Gander and his studio manager Alli Beddoes; Lamia Joreige; The Martin Z. Margulies Collection and curator Katherine Hinds; Emanuel Licha; Maria Barnas, Maxine Kopsa, and Germaine Kruip of Missing Books; Magdalena Sawon, director of Postmasters Gallery; Francesca Kaufmann and Chiara Repetto of Galleria Francesca Kaufmann; Michael Rakowitz; Liisa Roberts; and Hito Steyerl.

Sincere appreciation is due to Lionel Bovier of JRP|Ringier, our distinguished co-publishers; to the designer, Gilles Gavillet; and to copy editor Annie Lux. Within iCI, virtually everyone contributed something to the production of this exhibition. Initiated with the early encouragement of Judith Olch Richards, former executive director, this project was immediately supported by Kate Fowle, the new executive director, who began work during the most intensive phase of the project's development. Additional iCI staff members who deserve thanks include Frances Wu Giarratano, exhibitions manager, who shouldered the lion's share of the exhibition coordination with impeccable professionalism and skill, keeping the whole project moving and on schedule during a period of significant institutional transition; Kathryn Martini, registrar, for safeguarding the works throughout the exhibition and ensuring their proper presentation with total commitment; and the many other individuals whose work has led to the project's success: Renaud Proch, deputy director; Chelsea Haines, public programs and office manager; Kristin Nelson, development manager; Maia Gianakos and Sarah Thomas, former curatorial assistants; and iCI's interns Maggie MacTiernan, Pilar Pertusa, Beth Huffer, Ana Wilson, Maddie Keen, and Greg Barton.

For an institution like iCI, it is not only the rewarding work with guest curators that typifies our collaborative nature, it is also the interaction with the network of museums that present the exhibition in vastly differing contexts and to different audiences that further enriches the dialogue. We send thanks to all our colleagues on the tour for their crucial role in presenting *The Storyteller*.

Finally, on behalf of all my colleagues on iCI's staff, we extend our deep appreciation to our Board of Trustees for their continuing support, enthusiasm, and commitment to iCI's activities and programs.

—Susan Hapgood,
Director of Exhibitions

Exhibition

EXHIBITION FUNDERS
The exhibition, tour, and publication are made possible, in part, by grants from The Andy Warhol Foundation for the Visual Arts; the Horace W. Goldsmith Foundation; iCI Benefactors Agnes Gund, Gerrit and Sydie Lansing, and Barbara and John Robinson; and the iCI Partners.

EXHIBITION ITINERARY*
Salina Art Center
Salina, Kansas
October 22, 2009–January 3, 2010

Anna-Maria and
Stephen Kellen Gallery
New York, New York
January 29–April 9, 2010

Art Gallery of Ontario
Toronto, Ontario, Canada
June 9–August 29, 2010

Museo Nacional Centro de Arte
Reina Sofía
Madrid, Spain
July 7–18, 2010

(*at time of publication)

Editors' Acknowledgments

Claire Gilman and Margaret Sundell
would like to thank the many family
members and friends who generously
offered their advice and support in
the realization of this project:
Carlos Basualdo
Sally and Tim Brown
Jean Castelli and Lisa Silver
Joan Hardy Clark
Hannah Feldman
Gabriella De Ferrari
Priscilla Green
Alexander Greenawalt
Kent Greenawalt
Jessica Jenkins
Reinaldo Laddaga
Kathleen Madden
Roxana Marcoci
Doris Muir
Lynn Nesbit
Tricia Paik
Joanne Ramos and Dave Thomas
Thomas and Blaire Ritchie
Carol Ruderman
Jordin Ruderman
Susan Sollins
Nina and Michael Sundell

Publication

Series' Editor: Lionel Bovier
Publication Editors: Claire Gilman
and Margaret Sundell
Publication Coordinator: Frances
Wu Giarratano
Copy Editors: Annie Lux,
Clare Manchester
Design: Gavillet & Rust, Geneva
Typeface: Hermes-Sans (optimo.ch)
Production: Musumeci S.p.A.,
Quart (Aosta)

Cover: Steve Mumford, *3B2, Bathers by the Tigris River, Baghdad. The soldiers, from the Florida National Guard's 3/124th infantry, were looking for weapons caches.* (from the series *Iraq, 2003–2005*), 2003 (detail)

Photo Credits: Unless otherwise noted, all images are courtesy of the artists; cover, p. 62–66: courtesy Postmasters Gallery, New York; p. 11: courtesy Missing Books; p. 14–16: courtesy Cine Plus, Berlin; p. 20, 22–24: courtesy Greene Naftali, New York; p. 33–35, 38, 100, 102: photos by Martin Jenkinson; p. 41, 95: courtesy Francesca Kaufmann, Milan; p. 43, 44, 46, 97: courtesy Cao Fei and Lombard-Freid Projects, New York; p. 49, 50: courtesy Annet Gelink Gallery, Amsterdam, photo by Ilya Rabinovich; p. 52: courtesy Mounir Fatmi and Lombard-Freid Projects, New York; p. 57, 58, 60: courtesy Michael Rakowitz and Lombard-Freid Projects, New York; p. 70: © Magnum Photos

ISBN 978-3-03764-086-9

Co-published by
JRP|Ringier
Letzigraben 134
CH-8047 Zurich
T +41 (0) 43 311 27 50
F +41 (0) 43 311 27 51
E info@jrp-ringier.com
www.jrp-ringier.com

ICI (Independent Curators International)
799 Broadway, Suite 205
New York, NY 10003
Tel: 212 254 8200
Fax: 212 477 4781
info@ici-exhibitions.org
www.ici-exhibitions.org

In the same series:

ANDREA BELLINI (ed.)
Collecting Contemporary Art
ISBN 978-3-03764-015-9

MALCOLM MCLAREN (ed.)
Musical Paintings
ISBN 978-3-03764-058-6